Land Rover
Buying & Selling Manual

First published in October 2006

British Library Cataloguing in Publication Data:
A catalogue record for this book is available from the British Library

ISBN 1 84425 336 8

Library of Congress catalog card no. 2006924144

Published by Haynes Publishing, Sparkford, Nr Yeovil, Somerset BA22 7JJ, UK
Tel: 01963 442030 Fax: 01963 440001
Int. tel: +44 1963 442030 Int. fax: +44 1963 440001
E-mail: sales@haynes.co.uk
Website: www.haynes.co.uk

Haynes North America Inc.
861 Lawrence Drive, Newbury Park,
California 91320, USA

Printed and bound in Great Britain by
J. H. Haynes & Co. Ltd, Sparkford

All photographs supplied by the author
Front cover photograph by James Mann, with special thanks to
Rudkin Vehicle Services (www.rvslandrovers.co.uk)

Land Rover
Buying & Selling Manual

Haynes

How to do the best deals

Les Roberts

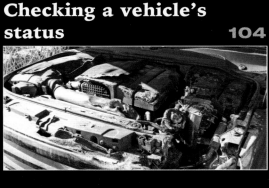
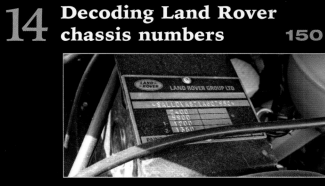
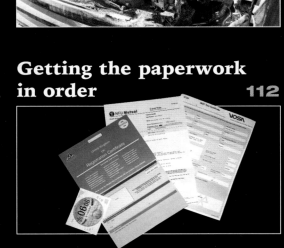

Introduction

The process of obtaining a Land Rover and disposing of your previous vehicle may seem to be quite straightforward, but getting the best deal from both a personal and a financial point of view and doing it with the least inconvenience and stress to yourself and your family requires that things be thought out in advance and planned with almost military precision. In order to enjoy happy, continued Land Rover ownership you need to ask yourself some pretty soul-searching questions and answer them truthfully, and then be prepared to listen to your head and not follow your heart.

You need to look at your finances and see if you can afford to pay for it in the long term as well as the short term, as ownership of this sort of vehicle is more expensive than a normal car in all areas – purchasing, running, insuring and fuelling. You also need to ensure you choose the right vehicle for your specific needs, as the Land Rover product range covers a diverse variety of four-wheel-drive vehicles spanning almost 60 years of production. Likewise, if you need to sell your Land Rover there are ways of doing this that will reduce the stress and maximise the return.

There are many books and magazines that cover most aspects of Land Rover vehicles, from history to classics, and off-road driving to adventure, with a healthy dose of DIY thrown in for good measure. You can enjoy all of these facets of ownership either as a participant or as a voyeur looking in from the outside. But there's one aspect that you usually experience only as a participant, though no help or training is usually received in the

OPPOSITE
The author's first
Land Rover,
purchased in 1973

LEFT
The author managed
to find and restore the
second oldest
existing Range Rover

subject. That is buying or selling your vehicle. Over the last 40 years I have bought and sold several thousand vehicles through the course of my employment, business and hobby, the majority being Land Rover products. I guess in total it's about 3,000 vehicles, and as each vehicle has involved both processes that makes a total of 6,000 transactions. These include buying my very first car, an Austin 7 Ruby (which I still own), for £7 10s in 1963 at the age of seven, and my first Land Rover, bought for £45 in 1973 and sold a few years later at a profit, to be repurchased more than 20 years and 11 owners later to restore and keep.

Trained as an engineer, I've never regarded myself as a salesman, even though I've sold more vehicles than many salesmen do in their entire career. I regard myself as a motor engineer, with car sales as just one facet of that business. I have, over the years, learnt a lot about the buying and selling process and even the maths and the science behind it. I now buy only a few vehicles per year and sell even less, as part of my hobby of restoring and collecting classic Land Rovers. Whilst most deals go according to plan some don't, and probably more has been learnt from analysing these than anything else. I feel it's now time to share my knowledge and hope it helps more deals, at all levels of the Land Rover market, to proceed as smoothly possible.

This book is intended to help the first-time buyer and the regular purchaser alike find the most appropriate way to buy and/or sell a Land Rover, and to ensure that they make the best deal they can in the process.

Les Roberts
Staffordshire 2006

Acknowledgements

I'd like to thank several people for their help, support and encouragement in the production of this book, firstly and especially my wife, my family and my friends, many of whom have been unpaid proofreaders. I'd also like to thank Richard and Cathy Howell Thomas at *Land Rover Monthly Magazine* for their help with this particular project and their encouragement to first 'take up the pen' back in 1988; the staff at Brightwells, Stable Motors, and Hunters of Derby for allowing me to use their vehicles and premises for photographs; and the staff at Haynes Publishing, in particular Mark Hughes and Steve Rendle, for having the faith to support this unique publication, and finally Derek Smith for his patience editing the final manuscript.

OPPOSITE
This Belgian built Minerva was imported and restored and satisfies the author's desire for something completely different

LEFT First step in buying vehicles, 1963

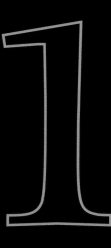

Buying

Identifying the need and separating 'need' from 'want'

The process of buying a vehicle satisfies one of our most basic instincts, that of the hunter gatherer, which in times past involved the hunt, the chase, and the kill and was predominantly a male occupation. Looking for a vehicle, weighing it up, and then securing it by driving a hard bargain involves much the same process.

The hunter gatherer's female was doubtless more in touch with reality and probably sent him out with the instruction: 'Fetch me a woolly mammoth for tea and don't come back with a rabbit,' as she knew that a woolly mammoth would feed the whole family for days. Likewise with vehicles, it's often the female partner in a family who actually makes the best car-buying decisions, as she probably has a better idea of what's genuinely needed and how much the family can afford than the male who does the legwork to get it. All purchases therefore need to be acceptable to all parties involved, so ensure you include your partner in the buying process right from the start if applicable in your circumstances.

Land Rovers by their very nature tend to be family vehicles, but if you're single you can buy whatever takes your fancy without being accountable to others, though it still does no harm to run your ideas past a friend first, as they may spot some significant factor that you may have missed. Whatever your circumstances you need to buy the most appropriate vehicle for your current and future needs, and it needs to be affordable. You therefore need to do a bit of forward planning.

The first thing to do with any vehicle purchase is the homework. You need to establish what it is you're going to buy, sort out your sources of funding, and resolve how you intend to pay for it. Only then should you start to hunt for the vehicle. Most purchases end up as some sort of compromise, and in the case of Land Rovers there might have to be several areas of compromise. We all want a vehicle that returns 50mpg at 100mph, doesn't depreciate, and will climb Mount Everest with a 3.5-ton trailer in tow and with seven people on board, but unfortunately it has yet to be made.

The process of deciding on what Land Rover product is best for you – or even if it should be a Land Rover at all – is best done at home, away from the pressure of a sales environment, and it's easiest done with a pen and paper. List all the realistic things you *need* the vehicle to be capable of and place them in order of priority. For example, if you do high mileages put the sort of mpg figures you need to achieve. Put the maximum and minimum passenger capacity you'll need. Put the towing requirement down, since if – for example – you wish to tow more than two tons this will rule out some of the product range. Put your budget figure down, and a realistic figure for the part-exchange value of your current vehicle if appropriate. Put down the rate of depreciation you're prepared to suffer, especially on more valuable vehicles, as a sum invested in a new vehicle will lose money more quickly than the same sum invested in a second-hand one. Then list all the things that you *want* as a secondary list. This is the list where the major compromises will probably have to be accommodated.

You need to clearly understand the difference between *need* and *want*. A *need* is a requirement or a necessity, and comprises the basic functional aspects of the vehicle you seek, including such things as diesel engine, four-wheel drive, automatic gearbox, tow bar, etc. You need to be clear and truthful in listing your needs. Most people who buy Land Rovers might *want* four-wheel drive, for example, but very few actually *need* it. There's no problem with this, as the world would be a very dull place if we all just satisfied

OPPOSITE
Not everyone needs to tow 3.5 tons like this, but most Land Rover products will do so

LEFT For some people automatic transmission can be a 'need', for others a 'want'

our basic needs, but you do need to be clear in your own mind. It's a bit of soul-searching really, and you might be surprised at your own answers!

A *want*, on the other hand, is something you long for, covet, crave, or desire. Wants might include leather seats, supercharged V8 engine, alloy wheels, shiny black paintwork, and a super sound system, or even the Land Rover itself, or a specific model within the Land Rover product range. You might want something that shows off your perceived status or even something that hides it.

Once you've identified your real requirements and entered in the price function as well then it's easy to dismiss quite a large selection of vehicles and distil down the essence of the specific type of vehicle that's best for you. In many cases there'll be more than one type of Land Rover that will fulfil your needs, and then personal decisions of what you *want* can come into play. A Defender 90 will fulfil most people's *need* list, but you might

BELOW A 90 stationwagon would satisfy almost everyone's 'needs' but not 'wants'

ABOVE There is nothing wrong in wanting a Range Rover Sport as long as you realise it is not a 'need'

BELOW Classified advertisements are a good place to start the hunt for a private sale vehicle

prefer to buy a Range Rover Sport, as that could fulfil your *need* list plus your *want* list too. In an effort to help you with this homework process I've included a crib sheet that you can photocopy and fill in (see Appendix 2).

Finding the vehicle

Once you've identified more clearly the type of Land Rover you want and the sort of price you'll be spending it's much easier to identify places that are likely to have such a vehicle on offer. You

need to decide what you're going to do about your existing vehicle, especially if you're intending to trade it in as part of the funding for the replacement. If you do intend to trade it in this will limit your sources for the replacement vehicle, as not everyone will want it. It might not be welcomed even by trade outlets, or you could be offered an unrealistically low price.

Trading your vehicle in will obviously limit you to dealing with people who trade, and they can be found advertising in local newspapers. Most regional evening papers have a specialist motoring section one night a week, traditionally on a Friday. There are also the free papers, and take a look at weekly publications such as *Auto Trader Magazine*, *Farmers Weekly*, and *Farmers Guardian*. Monthly publications are also useful, but the specific vehicles advertised might well have been sold. The most useful monthlies are the four Land Rover magazines, including *Land Rover Monthly*, but other ones have classified sections. Even if horses aren't your thing, *Horse and Hound* might carry an advert for exactly the model of Land Rover that you're looking for.

The internet is another good source of leads, either on the web pages of magazines such as *Auto Trader* or on internet auction sites such as eBay. Car auction companies also usually post a list of the cars they'll be offering a few days before the actual sale. They also post lists of sale prices previously achieved, so are a good resource for checking values.

If your vehicle requirement is a bit more specialised the various clubs have lists of vehicles for sale in their club magazines, which are a good starting point. Club members also often know of suitable vehicles available that have not been advertised and will possibly put you in touch with a potential vendor.

Another good source of leads is word of mouth. An owner of a similar vehicle will often recommend where they purchased it from and it's worth taking note of their comments, especially as they're just as likely to tell you about a bad buying experience as a good one. Even if you don't find the exact vehicle advertised you can build up a list of people and companies that sell similar ones, and you could call or visit them to see if they have what you're looking for. If you're determined regarding the attributes of your intended purchase you might have to travel quite some way to find the vehicle of your dreams. In the UK vehicles of a given age are generally cheaper if you head northwards and in better condition if you head south.

All these sources will eventually lead you to one of six sales environments: private vendors, auctions, internet auctions, specialist dealers, non-specialist dealers, and franchised dealers.

Private sales are one of the cheaper places to buy, or they ought to be if the vehicle is priced correctly; but human nature rules, and many people are greedy or are trying to get dealer prices without offering the services that dealers are legally or morally obligated to provide. It's also hard to deal with a private individual who isn't used to selling, and there's a great risk of buying a dud – the phrase *caveat emptor*, buyer beware, is particularly relevant here. Also, beware of traders trying to pass themselves off as private individuals.

A genuine private sale will offer you the opportunity of buying a vehicle for the lowest price possible and give you the maximum opportunity to inspect and test the vehicle before making the decision to buy. Most people won't want to take a part-exchange, though, and be prepared to look past the mud on the outside and the toffee papers on the inside to see the vehicle itself.

Auctions are another source of realistically priced vehicles. Land Rovers may be found either mixed in with normal vehicles in a general car auction or alongside other 4x4s at a specialist auction. They also often crop up in farm dispersal sales and at collective farm sales. There are only two sorts of vehicle at an auction: peaches and lemons. The peaches are there because they don't fit the sales profile of the dealer to whom they were traded in, who therefore sells them off to recoup his money. They're usually sent to auction because they're more than three or four years old, have done more than the expected average mileage of 12–15,000 per annum, or simply because the dealer has more vehicles than he can cope with – this is often the case just after new registration numbers come out. Leasing companies often dispose of their vehicles this way when the end of the leasing period comes up, while public companies and municipal users tend to auction their vehicles to achieve a fair price and accounting transparency. Many government vehicles, including army ones, are likewise auctioned, though often this is through a complicated tendering process in which it's difficult for a private individual to buy one vehicle. Private vendors might also auction their old vehicle so that they can buy another one without being lumbered with a trade-in. Most auctioned vehicles

ABOVE The specialised 4x4 auctions are clean, bright and good buying environments and not the grimy bombsite many people imagine

ABOVE The internet is another good source of privately offered vehicles

BELOW Beware of descriptions as one man's heap of junk is another's priceless historic artefact and the reverse is also true

up. These vehicles are offered with no warranty at all other than a guarantee of good legal title and are usually entered by various sections of the motor trade disposing of unwanted vehicles.

Be aware, though, that although all lemons are offered without a warranty not all vehicles without a warranty are lemons, as there may be another explanation. It might just be a company policy, or a perfectly good vehicle that's unwarrantable because it's a finance repossession or a Customs and Excise or Bailiff seizure. Unwarranted vehicles fetch less money at the fall of the hammer so it's entirely up to you to sort out if an unwarranted vehicle is a good buy or goodbye to a load of your money!

An internet auction on a site such as eBay is a sort of blend between a private sale and a regulated auction with no safety net in place. Whilst it's theoretically possible to sort things out if the vehicle is inaccurately described or has some other undeclared defect, in practice it's hard to do so. There's also no guarantee that the vendor has good legal title to the vehicle. Internet auctions are, however, a rich source of more specialised Land Rovers such as Series I, II and 101. Don't get carried away, though, as they always look better in the pictures than they do when you get them back home, and even the knowledge that someone else was prepared to pay one bid less than you doesn't mean that it's worth the money. eBay is also a good source of 'barn finds' and

will be offered with a warranted description, and if the vehicle isn't as described you can usually return it within a short, fixed time period.

The lemons, by contrast, are in auctions because there's a problem with them. It may be because they need a load of money spending on them to pass an MoT, or because there's a mechanical fault such as a slipping clutch or head gasket or some other major problem that isn't readily apparent as it drives through the auction hall. In fact you're lucky if you see it move at all, as many vehicles are auctioned as they sit parked

other project vehicles if you're interested in restoring something. It has a lot of good things for sale for sensible money, but you need to be very, very careful.

The popularity of Land Rover products has meant that there are quite a number of dealers and/or repair businesses specialising in them. These offer a great range of vehicles, the legal protection in buying from a dealer, and often other dealer facilities such as part-exchange and finance. They usually have well-presented vehicles on offer and tend to be genuinely enthusiastic about the product. They're mostly small traders keen to protect their reputation, so although some vehicles might turn out to be troublesome they'll not knowingly sell you a rogue, as it isn't in their interests to do so. There's usually far less sales pressure on the purchaser too. Their vehicles will be slightly more expensive than from other sources, as they have businesses to run and overheads to fund, but they'll be better presented and you can usually drive and test and inspect them as much as you want. Most of them will be either the dealer's own part-exchange vehicles, or else sourced from auctions or direct from main dealers to whom they've been traded in.

Appropriate vehicles can also be found for sale in non-specialist outlets. With the increasing popularity of 4x4 vehicles many car sales businesses and car 'supermarkets' have Land

Rover products on offer. They don't have the specialist knowledge but they're good places to buy, especially if you're intending to trade in a car or a non-Land Rover 4x4, as you'll probably get the best price for it here. They usually give warranties and offer finance. But if you're not familiar with Land Rover products the staff won't have the same knowledge as a specialist dealer and won't be as able to help you buy the correct type of vehicle suited to your needs, and you may even get steered towards something they just happen to have in stock.

ABOVE Auctions can offer the greatest savings so long as you understand the risks

BELOW Independent dealers carry a broad range of Land Rovers and other 4x4 vehicles, offering good quality at reasonable prices

RIGHT Land Rover
franchised dealers
have a full range of
well presented, quality
vehicles up to just a
few years of age

BELOW
Their showrooms
provide convivial
surroundings in which
to spend your money

Franchised Land Rover dealers offer the gold standard in Land Rover sales. They offer vehicles that in most cases have passed a rigorous series of tests and are sold within the manufacturer's 'approved vehicle' scheme. Usually these are high quality vehicles that have been traded in either to that specific dealer or to another dealer within the same franchise. Such dealers don't usually buy vehicles in to sell them on again, so most such second-hand stock is usually the result of a new vehicle sale. Exceptions include ex-Land Rover company-run vehicles such as press demonstrators, show vehicles, and vehicles run by the Land Rover dealership themselves.

The vehicles on offer from franchised dealers aren't the cheapest available but they're well presented and good quality. Consequently you'll not find much on offer over four years old, if even as old as that. You do have the reassurance that the vehicles will have been regularly serviced according to the manufacturer's schedule, will usually be of warranted mileage, won't have been heavily crashed in the past, and will have proper legal title. The dealer will also look within the stock of other franchised dealers for a vehicle that suits your requirements if they don't have the model that you need or want themselves. They might well run a demonstrator of a similar type to the one you're thinking of that you can test-drive, or sometimes even borrow for a few hours to ensure it's the right type of vehicle for you. They also provide you with the opportunity to test-drive other sorts of vehicle than the one you may be specifically seeking.

Making contact

The first point of contact between vendor and potential purchaser is often the telephone. If the vehicle is offered by a business then a personal visit is often best but it's still wise to telephone first and arrange a fixed appointment to view. This ensures that the vehicle is available to look at properly and is ready to test-drive. Some dealers have restricted space and several vehicles may need to be moved before the one you're interested in is accessible. Whilst it's a good idea to see the engine perform a cold start a proper business isn't going to sell you a bad starter as you'd be back on the phone the very next day, so at a dealer – but not elsewhere – you can take it as read that it starts, and you don't need to worry about a warm engine when you first meet the vehicle. If you're phoning a dealer have the vehicle details to hand, as they may have several of each sort for sale. Something like 'I'm interested in the red W reg Discovery' will ensure you're talking about the same vehicle.

When buying from a private individual it's best to phone and put a little test in place. Never disclose what vehicle you're calling about or where it's advertised, or even that it's a Land Rover. The statement 'I'm ringing about the car for sale in the paper' will result in one of two sorts of response: 'Oh the Discovery' or 'Which one?' The first is a sign that it's probably a private sale while the second indicates that it may be a non-disclosing trader, in which case it may be wise to move on down your list. Even if you're satisfied that it really is a private sale don't reveal any of the advertised details. Get them to say it's red and tell you that it's done 20,000 miles. A trader may have a green one as well that's done 40,000 miles and would have to do some quick thinking to keep up the pretence.

When you make the call you need to have the advertisement in front of you and a notepad and pen. If you're not confident on the telephone write a list of the things you want to ask, including things in the advert that need clarifying. Start with the important things that may or may not be in the advertisement, such as registration letter, exact colour ('red' may mean post-box red or a nice rich burgundy metallic), and exact model and trim specification, as the difference between them can significantly affect the value. Ask about the mileage and what sort of service history comes with it. Has the camshaft belt been changed if appropriate to that type of engine? If it's a recent vehicle ask if it's had all the manufacturer's recalls for safety-related items. Has it had any accidents or been an insurance total loss at any point in its life, not just during the vendor's ownership? Has it had any major expenditure recently or is any due? Ask how good the tyres are and if they're of an off-road pattern. Ask if it's been modified in any way, especially in one that might affect your insurance.

Ask if it's the seller's property and if their name is on the registration document. You need to ask them other things as well that may seem irrelevant at the time but can be used to judge if the vendor is truthful or not when you view the vehicle. Ask how long they've owned it, store the knowledge, and confirm it later when you see the registration papers, as they'll have forgotten what they told you. Ask what the vehicle has been used for and what the owner does for a living, and try to build up a picture of the vehicle and the vendor in your mind. If they both 'feel' right then arrange a viewing. If you delay matters the vehicle may well get sold to someone else, so move on quickly.

ABOVE All purchases should start here with some serious research as failure to do this will give less than perfect results

ABOVE Get detailed descriptions on the phone. 'Red' can mean a nice metallic burgundy like this or a completely different pillar box colour

FAR LEFT AND LEFT Be aware that your intended purchase may have a history the vendor is trying to hide from you

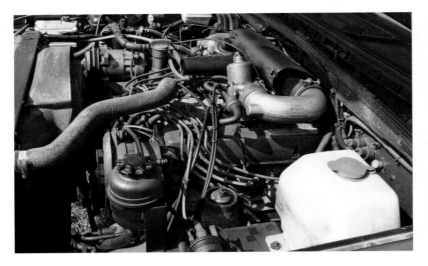

ABOVE If you are not familiar with this view then take someone with you who is

ABOVE RIGHT Vehicles like this do not really need a detailed survey. They will have been inspected already and approved by Land Rover. The resulting paperwork will be there for you to read

OPPOSITE TOP Independent dealers will usually allow detailed inspections by one of the motoring organisations or other competent person

OPPOSITE BOTTOM Most auction vehicles are sold with a declaration of no major mechanical faults and the rest you can inspect as it drives through the ring

Viewing

Danger warning: most people decide they want to buy a vehicle within the first 30 seconds of looking at it, and probably before they've test-driven it!

Viewing should be tackled in stages, and once you've found a valid reason to reject a vehicle you should continue no further. It's pointless, for example, to examine a vehicle in minute detail if it's red and you'd never buy a red car. It's also a waste of time looking at a 150,000-mile example if – no matter how tidy it looks despite the mileage, or how reasonably priced it is – concerns about its reliability and higher repair bills mean that you'd reject the vehicle anyway.

Always try to view the vehicle at the business premises of a trade vendor or the home of a private vendor, though it's acceptable to view it at the work location of a private vendor if, for example, lunchtime is more convenient for both of you. If a dealer wants to come and demonstrate a suitable vehicle to you then let them do the running, but only if it's really suitable. A private vendor may also offer to come to you, but this should only be done at your request, since checking the vendor's home address against the details in the paperwork is much easier if you're actually there.

Always view the vehicle from the standpoint that you're going to be its owner until you find reason (condition, cost, or circumstances) not to be. If you don't start with the intention of buying it then it's pointless looking at it at all and you're just wasting everyone's time, including your own. It's also a lot easier to spot negative points and give them their proper weight than to start unconvinced and have to find positive reasons to purchase it, as you'll put too much emphasis on tiny unimportant things just to convince yourself, and

possibly others, and may possibly miss more important reasons why you should be going home. But avoid adopting a 'buy at all costs' attitude, and take care not to give the vendor the idea that you'll buy it regardless, as you'll then have difficulty negotiating later.

If you're not confident with all the oily bits yourself then inspect what you can and pay someone else to do a full inspection. In many situations you can buy a vehicle provisionally on the basis that the deal will be finalised once it passes such an inspection, and most reasonable vendors will be happy with this. If they aren't, then move on. Though you'd think the reverse was true, in practice the less money you spend and/or the lower down the list of ideal sales environments you are then the more the vehicle needs to be examined. If you buy from a franchised dealer and spend several tens of thousands of pounds, then as long as the model specification and colour are OK, the tyres look good, and the service history looks fine then that's as far as you need to go. The vehicle will have had a comprehensive test before being offered for sale, and wouldn't be there unless it was a good vehicle. The dealer's business and the retention of their franchise depends on how they conduct their business, so you'll only find them selling 'honest' cars. Vehicles that don't fit their stock profile in terms of age and mileage or don't reach their exacting standards will be sold on within the trade and not put on the sales pitch.

When buying from a specialist dealer or non-Land Rover franchised dealer I'd suggest you only need to satisfy yourself about the vehicle's colour, specification, mileage, interior condition, service history, the way it drives, and the price, and if you're still happy at that point consider putting a returnable deposit on it and then arranging a professional check-over, either by one of the motoring organisations or by a genuinely knowledgeable person – even if you have a sound knowledge of vehicles it often pays to get an unbiased third party to inspect it for you! If you're happy with the outcome then continue with the deal. If problems crop up during the inspection get them resolved to your satisfaction before proceeding.

In an auction environment, get there early and identify potential purchases from the vehicles on offer. Examine the description, mileage, specification, etc. If you're happy so far then look underneath with a small torch and inspect the tyres and body in general. Wait until the vehicle's about to be brought through the ring, and when they unlock it look under the bonnet and listen when the engine is started. Follow it, and whilst the driver is in it look at the inside. Look for smoke and listen for noise as it drives to the rostrum. If you're still happy, then bid away. Remember that whilst you can reject a warranted car for an undeclared fault you can't reject it for something you might reasonably be able to see, such as a cracked light, a bald tyre, or a torn seat.

In an internet auction you're best advised to view the vehicle even if it involves travelling some distance. If the vehicle is only a few hundred pounds then it's probably safe to buy unseen, and if it's not as described then reject it when you go to pay and collect it. It's also safe to buy an expensive, quite recent vehicle for tens of thousands of pounds without inspection, since if it isn't exactly as described it's easy to reject. The problems come with middle-aged, middle-ground vehicles, where different interpretations are put on the description by vendor and purchaser. These are always best viewed before you bid.

By their very nature private sales will incorporate a viewing. First check that the initial asking price is reasonable (or only slightly above what you regard as reasonable) and that its specification, colour, mileage, etc, are acceptable. Then do a more detailed inspection. Again, don't go on once you've found a reason not to buy that can't be overcome. Some problems, such as a worn tyre, can be taken on board if the price is right, but you should walk away from such things as excessive corrosion. If you're not happy looking at the details yourself then take someone with you who has the required knowledge. The vendor will possibly reserve the vehicle for you pending the outcome of a professional inspection but will usually require a large cash deposit that might be hard to recover if you don't follow the deal through to completion.

RIGHT You can purchase a detailed status report from many sources between agreeing a deal and handing over the money. This is now much easier to obtain out of working hours using the internet

With all viewings and inspections, bear in mind that the vehicle isn't new and will show signs of wear. Also, look for positive points as well as negative ones. If you're comfortable with the idea of purchasing a specific vehicle you can move on to doing the deal, but if you're unhappy about it don't leave with a vague promise to think about it. Just tell the vendor straight that it's not for you. Be polite, and if they ask why then tell them. Whilst it's doubtful that you'll change your mind, a vendor might be prepared to revise his price in regard to condition, but if the problem you've found is insurmountable, or you're not at ease with the vendor, then don't waste time going on with the viewing.

There are only three reasons not to buy a properly researched vehicle that you've gone to view, and they're condition, cost, and circumstances – that is, if the vehicle isn't as described on the phone or in the advert, if it's too high a price, or if there's something wrong with the paperwork and/or you aren't happy with the vendor and the circumstances of the sale.

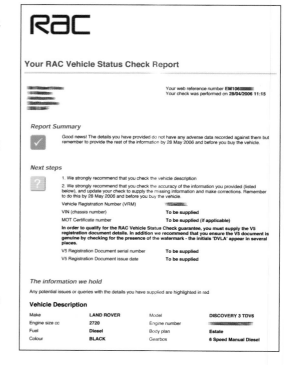

Your RAC Vehicle Status Check Report

Your web reference number EM106
Your check was performed on 28/04/2006 11:15

Report Summary

Good news! The details you have provided do not have any adverse data recorded against them but remember to provide the rest of the information by 28 May 2006 and before you buy the vehicle.

Next steps

1. We strongly recommend that you check the vehicle description
2. We strongly recommend that you check the accuracy of the information you provided (listed below), and update your check to supply the missing information and make corrections. Remember to do this by 28 May 2006 and before you buy the vehicle.

Vehicle Registration Number (VRM)	
VIN (chassis number)	To be supplied
MOT Certificate number	To be supplied (if applicable)

In order to qualify for the RAC Vehicle Status Check guarantee, you must supply the V5 registration document details. In addition we recommend that you ensure the V5 document is genuine by checking for the presence of the watermark - the initials 'DVLA' appear in several places.

V5 Registration Document serial number	To be supplied
V5 Registration Document issue date	To be supplied

The information we hold

Any potential issues or queries with the details you have supplied are highlighted in red

Vehicle Description

Make	LAND ROVER	Model	DISCOVERY 3 TDV6
Engine size cc	2720	Engine number	
Fuel	Diesel	Body plan	Estate
Colour	BLACK	Gearbox	6 Speed Manual Diesel

BELOW Whilst sometimes it is insisted upon, cash is not the best payment method except for small value purchases

Doing the deal

Having established that you're going forward with the buying process don't delay, as someone else might beat you to the vehicle or the vendor might

get bored by protracted negotiations. In some buying environments, such as an auction, you have to pay a deposit of, usually, £500 on the fall of the hammer and the balance within 24 hours, while some private vendors will pull out of an agreed sale if offered more money or a quicker completion. Whatever the environment in which you're purchasing the vehicle, after agreeing a deal you should move on as quickly as possible. The only valid reason for withdrawing after agreeing the deal is if something crops up when you're checking out the vehicle's legal status, as it isn't worth paying for a status check before knowing if a deal can be reached.

It's not just polite and good business practice to move on quickly, it's also in your best interests, as legal responsibility for the vehicle passes to you at the moment of sale. In an auction it's clear when this point of transfer basically occurs, as it's indicated by the fall of the hammer, or in the case of internet auctions by the finish time (though in practice it's at the moment of payment that an internet purchase becomes your responsibility, though you're legally obliged to complete the deal when won or agreed). In a person to person sale it's when the sale is agreed and, usually, finalised with a handshake, not when the money changes hands and the title is exchanged, which can be hours or days later but needs to be

kept to the minimum time possible. It's a bit like in a property sale, where the house becomes your responsibility for insurance and so on when contracts are exchanged, though it might be a couple of weeks later before you complete the deal and move in. You need to pay up as quickly as possible and take full possession rather than leave it in limbo. If the vehicle has a value of more than a few hundred pounds it's at this point that it needs insuring, and even if it isn't worth much it may still be worth insuring in case anyone makes a claim against the owner, who is legally now you.

Once you've agreed the deal sort out the method and timescale of payment and collection and ensure that it's mutually acceptable.

Taking it home

Never drive a vehicle on the road unless all the paperwork is in proper order and it's in a fit state to be on the highway. If it isn't fully legal it's much cheaper to have it delivered and to keep it off the road whilst you sort out the details.

To be legal it needs insurance. Your insurance company needs to be informed and cover needs to be arranged for that specific vehicle. You're not covered under the previous owner's policy or your own policy for other vehicles, as you own it even if it hasn't got your name on the V5 at this point. A phone call to your broker or insurance company in working hours will get you cover, as calls are time-logged. Out of hours it may be possible to get cover via the internet. You don't actually need the cover note in your hand. Note that the previous owner won't be insured to deliver the vehicle, as his cover ceased when you became the owner.

The vehicle also needs a valid MoT certificate unless it's less than three years of age, and a valid tax disc, which if you have proof of insurance and at least the green section V5C/2 of the logbook, plus a valid MoT, you can purchase at a Post Office that issues licences.

If all the paperwork is in order then check the vehicle is legal to use. Do all the lights work properly, are the tyres legal, and do the washers and wipers work? These items are all the responsibility of the driver, and just because it has a valid MoT certificate doesn't necessarily mean it's in a fit state to be on the road. The excuse that you've just bought it won't carry much weight with the police officer who's stopped you for a minor problem you could have seen for yourself. A bald tyre or non-operational light can be spotted by anyone, not just a mechanic.

LEFT Before you drive it home check that it is legal in respect of tyre tread depth and lights working etc. as it is now your responsibility and your driving licence at risk

Once you're happy all these things are correct make certain it has enough fuel in it to at least get you to a filling station. Bear in mind that fuel gauges are only a guide, and that some vehicles can run out whilst indicating that there's still fuel left. If in doubt take a can with you and put some fuel in yourself.

Finally, position the driver's seat and other controls to suit you if they're adjustable, and even the heater setting, as if you're unfamiliar with the vehicle the last thing you need is to be messing about with things while you drive it home! You also need to familiarise yourself with the basic controls, as they may be in different locations to what you're used to.

This is the culmination of a difficult and sometimes long and frustrating process. Bon voyage!

LEFT Take enough fuel with you to get to the nearest filling station, as the gauge may not be totally accurate. Otherwise pay the vendor extra to fill it up before you collect it

Selling

Identifying your marketplace

Selling ought to be the reverse of buying but in reality it's a lot harder. If I had the money I could go out today and buy say 25 or even more Land Rovers of all different types, but if I decided to sell my Land Rover today I'd be lucky to find one buyer in the next two or three weeks. It's a buyers', not a sellers', market, so to give your vehicle the best chance of selling you need to approach the task in the correct manner.

The first things to do are to quantify what it is you're actually intending to sell, and identify the proper market place for it. For example, I doubt if you'll sell your £40K Range Rover from a tatty postcard in a newsagent's window. Similarly, if you take a rusted-out Series III to a Land Rover main dealer on a trailer they won't give you money for it (though they might give you some to get it off their premises). Different vehicles have differing appeal so need to be marketed to the correct audience. In most cases if they're presented to the wrong audience there may be no one prepared to buy them at all. For example, there are very few people with available ready money to buy a vehicle worth several tens of thousands of pounds without recourse to a dealer's services in respect of part exchange, finance and warranty.

Land Rovers can be split up into groups in several ways. The most obvious method of division is by model type, but you can also differentiate them by value, age, and condition. It's these last three groups that determine the best marketplace for a specific vehicle, and they are dealt with in a separate section further on. Once you've worked out which classification method or methods are most applicable to your vehicle and taken on board such factors as the maximum price you might get, the length of time before the money would be available, and even the length of time between selling your vehicle and replacing it, it's time to work out your pricing structure and get it into the marketplace.

What should I ask for it?

Price and value might seem to be the same thing but they aren't. The value is the figure that you'd be happy to receive for your vehicle, which can be worked out quite easily with a little research as long as you're sensible. It's really the vehicle's true worth.

When it comes to establishing an asking price, different selling mediums need it to be lower or higher in order to achieve its perceived value. In a private sale environment, for instance, you need to ask for 110–115 per cent of its value, since people think that knocking the price down is the right thing to do and you'll therefore need a margin in which to manoeuvre. But don't be tempted to go in at too much over the odds, as this will put people off straight away.

Auction prices are lower, and even if you've been realistic with your value I'd suggest that you don't put a reserve on it of more than 90–95 per cent. It's a waste of your time and money to enter a vehicle that's not sold and the auctioneer will try harder once the reserve has been passed. If he considers the reserve to be unachievable he won't try at all but will just try to get it through the auction hall as quickly as he can and settle for the entry fee. However, if he thinks the vehicle's reserve is realistic then he'll try hard to sell it, as auction houses work on a commission basis. Payout is usually within a week, when you'll get the hammer price less commission. This is a quick way to sell a vehicle, but speed and lack of hassle have to be balanced against the lower figure realised if it only fetches its reserve price. But it may go for well over its reserve, in which case you'll be very happy.

Internet auctions are best tackled by a starting price of 50 per cent for lower value vehicles and 75 per cent or even more for higher values, with the reserve set at 100 per cent. If it sells for the reserve, then with selling fees taken into account you'll get more than 90 per cent of the

OPPOSITE You need to find the correct marketplace in terms of age, price and other special features of your vehicle

LEFT Auction sales usually return a lower sum to you than a trade-in or private sale, but it is a sale without hassle, quick and easy and often the difference can be recouped with a better deal on the replacement vehicle

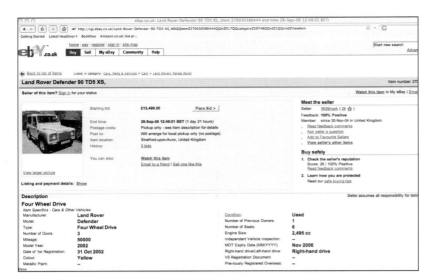

The eBay listing screenshot shows:

eBay.co.uk: Land Rover Defender 90 TD5 XS, (item 270030380444 end time 28-Sep-06 12:49:01 BST)

home | pay | register | sign in | site map   Start new search

Buy | Sell | My eBay | Community | Help

Back to list of items   Listed in category: Cars, Parts & Vehicles > Cars > Land Rover/ Range Rover

Land Rover Defender 90 TD5 XS,   Item number: 270

Seller of this item? Sign in for your status   Watch this item in My eBay | Email

Starting bid	£13,499.00	Place Bid >	Meet the seller
End time:	28-Sep-06 12:49:01 BST (1 day 21 hours)		Seller: 9939mark (26 ☆)
Postage costs:	Pickup only - see item description for details		Feedback: 100% Positive
Post to:	Will arrange for local pickup only (no postage).		Member: since 30-Nov-04 in United Kingdom
Item location:	Stratford-upon-Avon, United Kingdom		Read feedback comments
History:	0 bids		Ask seller a question
			Add to Favourite Sellers
You can also:	Watch this item		View seller's other items
	Email to a friend	Sell one like this		

Buy safely
1. Check the seller's reputation
   Score: 26 | 100% Positive
   Read feedback comments
2. Learn how you are protected
   Read our safe buying tips

Description
Four Wheel Drive
Item Specifics - Cars & Other Vehicles

Manufacturer:	Land Rover	Condition:	Used
Model:	Defender	Number of Previous Owners:	1
Type:	Four Wheel Drive	Number of Seats:	6
Number of Doors:	3	Engine Size:	2,495 cc
Mileage:	50000	Independent Vehicle Inspection:	--
Model Year:	2002	MOT Expiry Date (MM/YYYY):	Nov 2006
Date of 1st Registration:	31 Oct 2002	Right-hand drive/Left-hand drive:	Right-hand drive
Colour:	Yellow	V5 Registration Document:	--
Metallic Paint:		Previously Registered Overseas:	--

ABOVE Internet sites such as eBay are far from being risk free, but are a good way of offering your vehicle to a worldwide market and really good for rare or collectable Land Rovers

final figure, which ought to be satisfactory. If it sells well over the reserve price then you'll be pleased. Items sell much better when the people bidding see the reserve to be met and know that they stand a chance of owning the item, rather than keeping on seeing 'reserve not met' each time they bid, so I prefer to see items sold with no reserve but with the proviso in the description that you reserve the right to withdraw the item before the end of the sale as it's advertised elsewhere. If it gets to 90 per cent of the price you want by the last point at which you can withdraw it – usually 12 hours before the sale

finishes – then chances are it will go on to make the rest.

With a trade-in, if you're offered more than 90 per cent of its value I'd suggest you take it, especially if the price of its replacement is very competitive. You may be offered as much as 125 per cent of its value to tempt you to do the deal, but the extra will be factored into the price of the one you're buying.

Preparing it for sale

Before offering the vehicle for sale it needs preparing to look its best. As already mentioned, most purchasing decisions are made within the first 30 seconds of seeing a vehicle, and the rest of the viewing time and the test drive are to look for valid reasons to change that decision. It's actually a subconscious process and doesn't pass into the conscious part of the brain until later in the viewing process. If the decision in the first few seconds is *not* to buy, then virtually no amount of looking and testing will change this initial response. Obviously, then, it's the outside of the vehicle that needs the most attention, as this is the first thing that people see.

There are different levels of cleanliness appropriate to the different selling environments, and the preparation level expected by the purchaser in each particular environment needs to

RIGHT Do not overdo the preparation as honest dirt like this is better to see than a recently steam-cleaned engine bay and it saves you a job!

be right or else alarm bells start to ring, often subconsciously. Sometimes being too clean is as bad as not being clean at all.

If you're selling in a private sale, via an internet auction or an ordinary auction, or as a trade-in, then the vehicle needs to be clean and tidy but still have a look of careful usage. This is best accomplished by de-personalising the vehicle. Take all your spare CDs, coats, tools, and roadmaps out and make any changes – such as putting the original radio back in – before it's viewed. Clean the inside thoroughly but go easy on the polish, as you're not after too clean a vehicle. It's the same with the outside. Wash it off thoroughly and hose all the mud off underneath but go easy on the polish and the tyre black. Unless the engine bay is really filthy leave it alone. It's much better to see a slight amount of 'honest' dirt than a sparkly, steam-cleaned engine that might have had the evidence of telltale oil leaks or other problems cleaned off. If the vehicle is really bad and/or you can't do the work yourself have it professionally cleaned a couple of weeks before offering it for sale, so that the seats and carpets have time to dry and it starts to get a slightly used look again.

Dealers try to get a vehicle as near to 'as new' condition as they can. That's what their purchasers want and expect in a retail trading situation, but if you do so as a private vendor in anything other than a trade-in situation prospective purchasers think you're a dealer in disguise and

are hiding something about the vehicle's condition. As a trade-in your vehicle will be cleaned and prepared for onward sale anyway, so as long as it's reasonably clean you'll not get any additional money for the extra time you spend making it immaculate. It's hard work to clean a car to dealer standard without the proper chemicals and cleaning equipment.

Showing it off

When a prospective purchaser comes to look at your vehicle try to accommodate them as much as you can. Try to arrange a time that suits them, even if you have to change your own routine slightly. After all, you do want to sell your vehicle! Ensure it's in a usable, legal state for a test drive, ie taxed, MoT'd, and insured for you to drive. Though you might save a little money by cashing in the tax or insurance you'll find it very difficult to sell a vehicle that can't be driven or at least ridden in. Have some fuel in it. If it's a project, or has no MoT so it can't be driven on the road, at least have it in working order so that it starts and runs. Have the registration papers and current MoT handy for inspection, along with old MoT tests if available and any other paperwork, including invoices for servicing work or spare parts like tyres.

If you're auctioning your vehicle then once

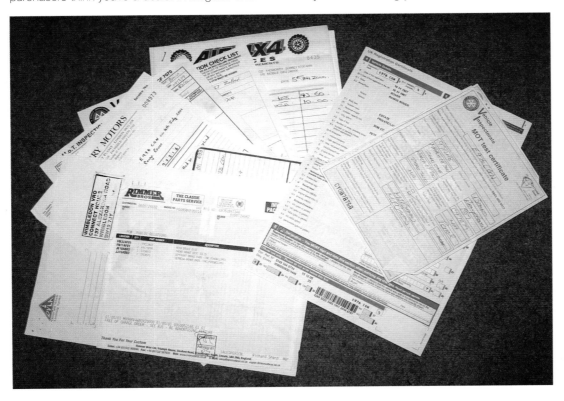

LEFT Have as much historical paperwork as possible to hand as it confirms mileages, service history and so on, and gives the impression of a caring owner

you've entered it in the sale it's out of your hands, but people interested in an internet sale will sometimes want to look at the vehicle before bidding. Treat these as a private sale without the deal bit at the end.

As a trade-in you have the disadvantage of undertaking the buying and selling processes at the same time. As they're really two different transactions going on concurrently you need to be particularly alert, especially as the excitement of obtaining a newer vehicle might result in you letting down your defences so that you end up with less for your old vehicle than anticipated – especially if you've not done your homework and established its proper value on the open market.

In a private sale allow potential purchasers all the time they need to look at the vehicle, and reply to their questions truthfully and in reasonable detail. Some people need a lot of time to make up their minds and are very wary whilst others are more impetuous, and there's a whole spectrum in between. They're all buying from you for one reason, and that's price. With Land Rovers the potential saving when buying privately applies to vehicles far older than when buying normal cars, since the specialist Land Rover trade will sell anything they can turn a profit on from 1948 onwards and in any condition, even project vehicles. With more recent vehicles, however, the potential purchasers are at your door because they've chosen to forego the cup of coffee in the showroom, the suited salesmen, and the all-embracing warranty experience just in order to buy the same item for less money.

Always keep the keys in your pocket, especially on high value vehicles, and don't let anyone else drive the vehicle unless your own insurance covers any driver. Don't let someone drive it under their insurance cover unless you see their policy and check that it's comprehensive and it states that it covers 'any vehicle the property of the policyholder or in their care custody or control', such as on a motor trader's policy. People think they're covered on their own insurance but often it's only third party and no use to you if they damage it before paying. Always accompany them for the drive and don't forget to lock your house. Unfortunately, lots of vehicles are stolen in a sale environment when the vendor isn't fully aware of the risk and isn't in control of the situation. This is especially important with high value vehicles fitted with sophisticated alarms and immobilisers, which are otherwise hard to steal.

You'll find that the cheaper the vehicle is, the more rigorous the inspection. It's just one of those strange anomalies of life. You'll generally find someone buying a Land Rover for £300 will look at it in much more detail than someone buying one for £30,000. Whatever the vehicle and price the method is the same: give them room and let them look, but judge when the right time has come to get more involved. There's no specific time to move in but it's usually when the looking finishes and the head scratching and musing starts. You have to watch the body language carefully and often it's when they come over to you that's the right time, as it signifies that they're ready to talk.

Doing the deal

If the purchaser is happy with the vehicle after a physical inspection and intends to go forward with the purchase process you need to agree a price and a timescale and method of payment that's acceptable to you both. Dealing with and handling money are both dealt with in other sections. You need to give the purchaser the opportunity of a professional inspection by one of the motoring organisations or their own 'man' if they so wish. More astute purchasers will also want to check the vehicle on the various databases for outstanding HP, accident damage and theft, but they'll probably do this between agreeing to buy the vehicle and paying for and collecting it. They might well want a photocopy of the V5, or will write down the VIN and registration details for this purpose. Don't get suspicious about their motives: they're just doing the correct thing.

Don't take the vehicle off the market without a cleared cheque or a big wad of cash as a deposit. I'd consider £200–£500 to be a reasonable amount. It needs to be a large enough sum that they're unlikely to walk away from if they develop cold feet. The motor auctions regard £500 as being the minimum deposit and will require it from you in cash or card payment within minutes of the hammer falling, in order to give the purchaser as little time as possible to go cold on the deal. Whilst a winning auction bidder has technically entered into a legally binding contract at the fall of the hammer the likelihood of this being successfully enforced is slim, in which case the deposit goes some way towards covering the auction costs if the sale doesn't go through.

If the purchaser in a private sale only tenders a small deposit in relation to the sale price then don't take it, and keep the vehicle on the market until they show up with all of the funds. That way you could still sell it to someone else if they want it and can pay quickly. Taking a small deposit just

LEFT Whilst shaking hands on a deal is a good gesture, it has no legally enforceable connotations

hinders you. People used to be more honourable in car dealing and a gentleman's word was his bond, but sadly this isn't true any more even amongst gentlemen, so only regard a sale as likely to complete if a minimum of £200 in cash backs up the buyer's word. This is the maximum some people can readily get out of a hole-in-the-wall cashpoint, or can scrape together at short notice for an evening or weekend viewing if they weren't geared up to go out and buy a vehicle. Bear in mind that someone who has set out to purchase a car and has drawn a worthwhile sum in readiness for the deposit is more likely to have sorted out where the rest of the money is coming from and how they intend to pay you.

Letting go

Seeing someone else drive off in what has been in some cases a major part of your life can have a few tugs on the emotional heartstrings, but to counter this there's that warm feeling you get from a big wad of cash in your pocket or a healthy-looking bank balance. But don't let the vehicle go unless you have the money in cash or the funds have cleared in your bank account, and don't let it go until anything that can be stolen, forged, bounced or stopped has been cleared by your bank. If the purchaser wants the vehicle in a shorter time frame, which is quite understandable, then get them to pay in a way that gets the money to you more quickly in a secure form such as an inter-bank transfer. If it's folding money then count it all and look at the notes carefully, as forged money is hard to spot when mixed with real money.

If you auction the vehicle then the auction house will pay out a few days after the sale and usually you're OK, though it's not unknown for them to go bust and then the vendor loses out. It's extremely rare, though. Treat internet auctions as private sales, as that's what they are, and get your money cleared before releasing the vehicle. Though payment through the PayPal system will cost you 4 per cent in fees it's guaranteed payment and might be worth the loss, especially if you've factored this extra amount into the figure you're happy to accept.

The only truly safe way to get rid of a vehicle is to trade it in, as you never see the actual money: it's just a paper figure debited off the amount you have to pay for the replacement, and you therefore don't have to worry about getting paid for it.

When the new owner picks up the vehicle give them a written and dated receipt (see Appendix 3). It's best if they sign it as well. Keep a copy and fill in the V5C registration document. Tear off their bits and don't forget to send the rest to the DVLA to relinquish responsibility for the vehicle. It's best to keep a photocopy of the bit you send, in case they mislay the rest of it and you need to prove it wasn't you who drove through the speed camera. It's also courteous to give a photocopy to the purchaser for their own records until the proper one reaches them. And that's the conclusion of a successful sale. All you have to do now is wave and wish them bon voyage as they drive off.

Finally, don't forget that you sold the vehicle in the state it was in when they viewed it, so you can't remove all the extras you've fitted unless their removal was part of the negotiated deal. It's also polite to leave enough fuel in to go a reasonable distance, at least to the nearest filling station.

Where and when to buy and sell

£0–£5K price range

With new vehicles costing in some cases more than £60K, Land Rovers for less than £5K are by their very nature the bottom end of the market. You'll not see any for sale at main dealers and will only find a limited number of them at independent specialists, as they're worried about repair and warranty costs. However, small one-man-band businesses do sell this sort of vehicle. They can also be found at auctions, but the high cost of selling them there means that they've usually come from big dealers who enter them in bulk at specially negotiated rates.

The usual haunt for this sort of vehicle is therefore the private sale, internet sale, or the sort of enthusiast part-time dealer who likes to buy and tidy up vehicles and sell them on to subsidise other areas of his hobby. You'll most likely find them in the local papers, trade papers such as *Auto Trader Magazine*, and such specialist Land Rover magazines as *Land Rover Monthly*. The *Auto Trader* website also has a large selection of vehicles in this sort of price range and, conveniently, tells you how far they are from your home. Internet auctions such as eBay are another ready source of such vehicles.

If you're selling in this price band it's appropriate to use similar mediums, and possibly several of them in order to reach as wide an audience as possible. The magazines are especially good for unusual vehicles as they have a wide enthusiast audience. There's a time delay between entering a vehicle for sale and it appearing in print, so this isn't an appropriate medium if you want it gone quickly, even though you'll probably get a better price and are less likely to be messed about than in an eBay sale. Be prepared for people to come and view the vehicle and for them messing you around and wasting your time by not appearing when arranged.

Local papers are good for advertising, both the evening and the weekly ones, and the time frame is much quicker than for magazines. Some will even put pictures in, and this helps a sale. You'll hopefully get multiple viewings so try to turn one of them into a sale. Once again, however, you will – not might – be messed about.

An auction will cost a lot of money in charges and entry fees to sell a vehicle, and the specialist 4x4 sales are the only place where it will fetch even a reasonable sum. And don't forget the delivery costs. If it sells, however, there'll be no comeback as long as the legal bits are right and you'll get the cheque a week later. You also don't get potential purchasers or time-wasters coming to your house to view the vehicle, and some people are happy to accept the lower price just to keep their privacy.

Auctioning on the internet has the advantage that it's at a fixed finishing point and if all goes well and it sells then you'll get paid a few days later. If you really need to sell something then a combination of several mediums will spread the exposure both over time and area.

£5K–£10K price range

The independent specialist dealer is probably the most ready source of vehicles in this price range and is probably the safest place to shop. As you reach the higher end of the price range you're heading away from the sorts of sums of money people have as ready funds, and often they have to borrow some while the rest is locked up in their current vehicle. Therefore a lot of people will be almost forced to use a dealer as they either don't have the funding available to buy another vehicle and then sell their own or else they need to use the finance arrangements a dealer can offer. Because this is their market sector such dealers will have a ready stock of such vehicles, so even if you don't need their facilities they're a good place to look.

If you have the funds available then good deals can be had at auction or on the internet, though

you need to be especially careful about the quality and especially the status of anything you decide to buy in this price range. Status-wise it's safe to buy at an auction and some houses will even provide written engineers' reports (at your expense) on vehicles you're interested in. If you have the funds and the technical expertise, or can import the expertise into the buying process, then you'll do as well at auction as anywhere else in this price bracket.

Internet auctions are another good source if you have the ready funds, as this puts you at an advantage over those who don't. However, as the vehicles get more expensive it's a lot of money to lose if you buy unwisely, as you don't have the safety net that's provided in a regulated auction site or at a registered dealer.

As a buyer, the private adverts in magazines and the local paper are a rich seam worth quarrying, since it's a buyers' market here as the number of people in a position to stump up the full cost are limited and you can often drive a hard bargain, especially if the vehicle has been for sale for a while and the owner needs to sell it. There's always the worry that being unsold for a while and the vendor's preparedness to knock 25 per cent off the asking price mean that it's a dud, but as long as it passes all the checks it probably means no more than that you're the first person to come

BELOW Whilst an independent dealer is not the cheapest place to buy, you do at least have some legal protection not applicable to a private sale

ABOVE Sought after models such as the 110 Stationwagon sell well in all environments if properly priced

along in a position to pay for it! There are very few people with £10,000 readily available, so if you're selling treat all enquiries respectfully, consider all offers carefully, and remember the old adage that a bird in the hand is worth two in the bush. You might think as a seller that your vehicle is worth £10K or even more, but having a 'live buyer' standing in front of you prepared to hand over £8,500 needs careful handling, as if you refuse you may not get a better offer. As a buyer with funds you need to use this advantage to your profit.

You're unlikely to find vehicles in this price range at a franchised Land Rover dealer, as they won't fit the stock profiles they operate, though you may possibly find a Freelander or basic 90 Defender at the top end of the band, as their cheaper initial cost means they fall just within their stock profile.

If selling it's probably easiest to trade in, as independent dealers will be looking for stock such as this and will give you a good price. If you go to a main franchised dealer it's easier to use your vehicle's value towards the replacement's cost, and even if they don't retail it again they'll have a

ready trade market. It will also sell well at auction, though possibly for less than you thought, but you'll have an uphill struggle to sell it from a classified ad or on eBay. Though you may seemingly get quite a lot of interest you'll have difficulty actually completing the deal. Some independent dealers will buy in vehicles directly and may be prepared to sell the vehicle on your behalf, which will return you a higher figure though you have to trust them to actually pay you when it's sold. They'll often be prepared to take and deal with another vehicle on your behalf in part exchange for yours, which gets round the main difficulty of selling vehicles of this value privately.

Though you'll have difficulty selling it through a classified advert, if time isn't critical you will match it to a new owner eventually so long as your asking price is realistic. If the vehicle is a sought-after model such as a 110 Defender County Station Wagon, or is genuinely rare, then it'll stand a much better chance of selling than if it's just another Discovery or Freelander. To sell easily from an advert it needs as much exposure over as big an area as possible

£10K–£15K price range

This is the true territory of the specialist independent dealer and it's the market area that they like to sell vehicles in all the time. You'll find lots of stock on offer and will probably not have to compromise much on your requirement list. Even if your exact requirement isn't available there's a good chance they'll know where a Land Rover suitable for your needs can be found and they'll often go to great lengths to get your business. The franchised Land Rover dealers also have a lot of stock on offer, especially Freelanders – as you head towards their list price new, so second-hand ones within the higher end of this price band will fit within the dealer's stock profiles.

As you'll probably have a cheaper vehicle you need to trade in you might be forced to go to one of these two sources. If your vehicle is relatively new or valuable then the franchised dealer is best, but if it's older and/or less valuable the independent specialist will be the better option, as you'll get a better deal, especially if they'll be able to retail your trade-in.

If you're lucky enough to have funds for a straight deal you'll do well at auction, and with private classified adverts if you can convince the vendor to take your low offer. If you want a straight deal at a dealer you ought to be able to get a price reduction, as they'll have built in quite a margin to blow on trade-ins. Auctions are a very good source of vehicles in this price band, since they're there because they don't fit the main dealers' profile or have come direct from a leasing company. If you're prepared to buy something a little harder to sell, such as a vehicle with a higher than average annual mileage, then you'll get an especially good deal at auction.

Selling privately becomes harder as the value goes up, and though you might succeed with a classified advert it'll be a long slog and you'll have to be competitively priced to get people interested, who'll then proceed to carve even more money off. It's doubtful, if you're selling one vehicle in this bracket and buying another, if you'll be able to do so at a lower total cost than if you traded the old one in against its replacement at a dealer. It would certainly be more fuss and aggravation.

If you need a straight sale then consider an offer from an independent dealer, who'll probably buy it, especially in better selling times, or will sell it on commission. If your vehicle is subject to a finance agreement they'll be able to buy the vehicle from you and pay it off and give you the balance, as will an auction house. This is really the only way to dispose of a vehicle on finance if you undergo a change in circumstances.

If you do use classified adverts be prepared for the disappointment of not receiving a single call. Spread your bets well, with shorter-term exposure in local papers and longer-term exposure in specialist Land Rover publications. You should even think about advertising in magazines such as *Farmers Weekly*, *Horse and Hound*, etc. You'll need a few hundred pounds as an advertising budget and you might spend it all without any result.

Internet auctions are dangerous, because as either a buyer or seller at this level – as in all dealing – there has to be an element of trust between both parties. It's much easier to trust a business that has fixed premises and a reputation to protect. It's harder to trust someone you've possibly never met and to part with money for a vehicle you've perhaps never seen.

As a vendor it's doubtful if you'll top the price offered as a trade-in or as a straight purchase by a dealer, and if it's a good quality vehicle it ought to make more in a normal specialist vehicle auction. There are very few people with this level of ready money and the only reason they'll be prepared to buy directly from you is if the vehicle is significantly cheaper than similar vehicles elsewhere or is an especially rare and unusual limited edition. Even then they won't want to pay over the odds. Only put a vehicle of this value on eBay if your acceptable sale price is undeniably cheap and then be prepared for it not to sell or for the winning bidder to get cold feet and vanish.

BELOW Independent dealers sell vehicles in most price ranges including vehicles outside the franchised dealer stocking critera of age and mileage

The reason it's difficult to sell privately in this price band in any medium is that as prices rise the number of people with ready money diminishes. People do buy vehicles of this value but they usually need to use their current vehicle as part of the funding process and a loan of some sort for the balance. As you don't want to take a part exchange and can't offer finance it limits the number of people in a position to deal with you.

As a purchaser internet auctions ought to be a place to buy if you have the money, for exactly the same reasons. Don't be tempted to pay anywhere near as much as you would to a dealer, as there's no warranty etc. Remember you're entering a legally binding contract to buy if you place a winning bid. If you're going to bid then it's best to view the vehicle and even have it inspected beforehand, as the only reason you can legitimately back out later is if the vendor doesn't have good title or has lied in the description or in answers to questions. It's best if you build a relationship with the vendor, preferably in person

or else on the telephone, as 'live' contact is best, but by email if you must. Internet auctions are a good way to be introduced to vehicles for sale, and when they don't sell – because either the start price or the reserve are set too high – you can approach the depressed vendor with a low offer afterwards and buy it as a normal private sale. Tread very carefully, though. and do everything you can to check out both the vendor and the vehicle.

£15K and upwards

This is the sort of price territory in which main dealers with expensive premises like to sell. The majority of the stock on offer will have been generated as trade-ins from the sale of new vehicles and will be around three years old or less. Such dealers have strict criteria regarding mileage, service history and condition, and most of their stock will have passed an inspection

BELOW The private vendor can not offer the same facilities as dealers in respect of finance, part exchange and warranties and so ought to be asking a lower price

procedure to become approved second-hand vehicles. A Land Rover franchised dealer ought to be offering a premium product and a premium service, all at a premium price. It's a simple buying experience, as all you need is a quick trip round the block and if you're happy you just give them the money. You don't need to check the vehicle, other than possibly to see if the tyres are good, as you can be certain it's not on finance or written off and it will have passed a comprehensive checklist before being offered for sale. You don't even need to open the bonnet.

You'll also find similar vehicles at specialist outlets, though they're unlikely to be as good as at a main dealership as they'll be above-average mileage or won't have a full main dealer service history or will have something else about them to put a main dealer off, though it may just be that they're too old for the latter to sell. They'll also be less expensive and may represent better value for money. It's a good idea to look the vehicle over a bit more carefully, ask a few more searching questions, and do a status check or request to see a copy of the one they'll have done.

If you need to trade your old vehicle in then it's only the two sorts of dealer that you can look to. You might fare better at a franchised dealer if your vehicle is good enough for them to retail, but though at the end of the day the figures written on the invoice may be higher, the difference between them – the balance needed to fund the replacement – will probably not be much if any more at the franchised dealer, so don't dismiss them on the grounds of price.

Auctions have a lot of good vehicles, especially ones that aren't main dealer stock. A two-year-old one with, say, 50,000 miles on the clock wouldn't be offered for retail by a main dealer as it ought to have done only 24,000, so it would probably go to auction for sale into or even directly to the non-franchised trade. Usually they're otherwise good vehicles. However, you'll have to fight with the independent dealers to buy such a vehicle, as this is where a lot of their stock comes from and they don't like private individuals muscling in on what they perceive as a trade resource. Try not to let on you're a private purchaser and especially an auction virgin or they'll run you up and skilfully stop bidding just before you do!

Private adverts do have vehicles for sale in this range but they're usually scruffy and/or overpriced as a greedy vendor tries to better the figure they've been offered as a trade-in. This offer may have been low because of the condition of the vehicle, but the vendor will still believe he can better it elsewhere. Buying or selling a vehicle of

this value from a private ad will only work if the vehicle is significantly cheaper than those of similar condition being offered elsewhere. I don't just mean a few pounds cheaper. A vehicle that might be at a main dealer for £20K or an independent for £18.5K will only sell if you're prepared to accept £16–£17K, and you might only get offers of £14–£15K if any at all. It also needs to be well presented, clean internally and externally, and have no reason to put someone

ABOVE AND BELOW
Only top quality recent vehicles will fit the exacting requirements of a Land Rover franchised dealer's previously-owned stock offered for retail sale

off buying it. If it needs paintwork repairs, valeting, a new tyre or light lens, or money spending on it in any other way you'll get really low offers at best.

As a buyer sitting on this much ready funding you're in a strong purchasing position, especially in a private sale, as you're a very rare commodity. Inspect the vehicle very carefully, go through the paperwork and status checks in depth, and go in with a really low price, bearing in mind the proportion of the prices quoted above.

If you're selling a vehicle of this value then it's easiest and safest to trade it in or sell it into the trade directly or at auction. If you have time and money to waste try classified adverts, but be prepared to tolerate dreamers, skinflints and time-wasters in the vain hope that there might be a genuine buyer among them, as you only need the one. Be wary, though – you might be targeted by rogues planning to either scam you or even to steal the vehicle, as you present a ready target and the higher value puts you at a greater risk. Likewise you may sell the vehicle on eBay, but it'll probably take several attempts and need relisting, and you need to be very aware that there's more chance of the deal failing to be completed than with a cheaper vehicle.

Trading your vehicle against another

The easiest way of getting rid of your old vehicle is to go to a dealer and trade it in against its replacement. The money side is easier as you only have to deal with the balance rather than the whole amount. It also simplifies the changeover process as you just drive in with one vehicle and out with the other. It avoids having two vehicles and laying out extra funds whilst you sell the other, or even having no Land Rover at all if you sell yours before purchasing a replacement. It's not always best financially, though, especially if your vehicle isn't one the dealer would readily sell on again.

It's only appropriate to try to part exchange a vehicle at a suitable dealer for that particular type. Private vendors generally won't be interested in a part exchange deal at all so it's not appropriate to ask them. The trade, however, will often take your vehicle, though there's no compulsion for them to do so and it may not be worth their while financially. If you have an old car (by 'old' I mean more than five years) most independent specialists won't be interested, though if you find a Land Rover amongst the stock of a general garage they may take it. Main dealers won't be interested in your 25-year-old Series III just because it has a Land Rover badge. They'll be interested in your two-year-old Land Rover, though, and even more recent vehicles, as they'll be able to move them on.

Don't assume a dealer will automatically want your vehicle or will give you a good price, or that this is financially the best way to get rid of it. It *is* the least hassle, though, and the ease of the transaction must be weighed against the possibility of getting a better price on the open market.

If you ask the dealer first you'll get an indication of your vehicle's value before you start looking at his stock for a replacement. This will save you wasting time chasing a deal that'll never happen.

Once a dealer has indicated he'll take your vehicle as part of a deal it all comes down to price. He may not offer what you think it's worth, but it'll be the auction value plus the margin that's been built in to the price of your replacement to 'blow' on a trade-in. If, on the other hand, your vehicle fits the dealer's stock profile and it could be sold on again you might do a bit better. Usually the deal you'll be offered doesn't leave much room to manoeuvre and you'll not be able to improve it much.

The secret is to look at the cost of swapping and not the actual figures for the two vehicles. It's easier for you to understand and an easier way for the two parties to deal. You're only dealing with one figure rather than trying to up the offer and lower their asking price at the same time. The sales person will have sized you up and by looking in the price guide will have worked out the minimum price he thinks you'll go for and then added a bit on for you to knock off. It won't be a lot, though, as most deals like this are quite lean from the outset. Ignore the actual prices and if you have a realistic valuation in mind for yours and a realistic value for the replacement, then as long as the difference is acceptable to you do the deal.

Because of the way VAT works with car sales the dealer will prefer to reduce the price of your vehicle trade-in on the invoice to avoid paying tax on what's actually only a paper profit and not a real one. So as long as the agreed price difference is still maintained don't be worried if they ask you if it's OK to put down different figures on the invoice. The trade-in price they use will probably be the same as they hope to get from selling it on within the trade, and as the tax is paid on the profit on the replacement vehicle the figures will probably be more realistic than the inflated windscreen price. As you're ultimately paying the tax it's to your advantage to accept the figures. It's not illegal, as they're merely reducing the invoice figure to a real level rather than the inflated one on the windscreen.

When you present your vehicle have it in the same condition as you'll be getting rid of it. Replace the original stereo, put back the original wheels, and clean it inside and out. It may seem a waste of time but it might make a few hundred pounds difference in its valuation if your Land Rover is seen as a clean, well cared-for vehicle. You can have a vehicle professionally cleaned for £75 or so and it would be well getting this done a few days before taking it for appraisal.

Market variations within the UK

Quite significant price variations can be found amongst similar vehicles depending on whereabouts in the country they're situated. This phenomenon isn't unique to the UK and occurs within most countries. There are even world variations, with many people making a living by buying one sort of Land Rover in one country and selling it at a profit in another. Within the UK the variation basically depends on how far north you're situated, though some might argue that it's really how far from London the vehicle is being offered for sale. There are model variations too within this geographical distribution, and these change according to the age and thus the value of the vehicle.

If you're prepared to travel you can sometimes use these price variations to save money, though the costs of travelling and retrieving the vehicle if you purchase it will eat up a big chunk of the saving. Most people like to buy a vehicle from a source as near to their home as possible but it really matters little where it was purchased, though warranty work – if you're unfortunate enough to need it, or lucky enough to get it – is easier at the sale premises, especially with a vehicle bought from a non-franchised dealer. Within the UK the value of an otherwise identical vehicle is a lot less as you travel north, so you're well advised to look in that direction if you're going to buy outside your home area. Prices are also cheaper as you head away from the middle of the country so are generally less in Wales and East Anglia. The variations actually follow the same pattern as house prices and average wages, though the percentage differences are less with vehicles. The variation in vehicle prices

has something to do with travelling time: it's difficult to get someone to travel for much more than an hour to view a vehicle, especially as several trips are often necessary before the vehicle is finally collected. So if there are many people living within an hour's travelling time of the vehicle it will sell more easily for a better price. If you don't mind travelling it's therefore worth looking at the more remote parts of the country, where the price will be lower and the vendor keener to move metal.

The desirability of certain models also changes across the country. Defender 90 commercial vans and Pick Ups are strong sellers in the farming areas of Wales, the Lake District, and the Peak District, as farmers like their smaller dimensions that enable them to turn off a lane into a field with a loaded sheep trailer easily; but a 90 Pick Up will be much harder to sell to someone who lives in the middle of London. A 110 Station Wagon, on the other hand, is a 'lifestyle' type of vehicle and sells better where there's more wealth, so is more suited to people living between the Midlands and the outskirts of London.

Markets also vary with the age of the vehicle.

People in the south and other centres of conurbation tend to spend a lot of time travelling to work and therefore usually run more recent vehicles and pay for repairs to be carried out elsewhere. In less affluent areas people tend to run older vehicles and, either by desire or necessity, do any repairs themselves. Thus a £50K Range Rover will find a buyer more easily in the centre of a big city and a £1,500 older one will sell better in the sticks or 'oop in the 'ills'. But these trends apply primarily to Land Rovers used as normal everyday vehicles. An enthusiast living in London might want a 90 Pick Up on which to fit a roll cage and other bits in order to play at weekends while a Scottish landowner might buy a £50K Range Rover, though both vehicles are likely to be sourced well away from the intended point of use. Discovery and Freelander Land Rovers also tend to migrate away from the bigger population centres as they get older and become sought after for their abilities rather than as lifestyle accessories.

Condition variations also occur within the UK. In general rust is the real vehicle killer, and that has a direct correlation to the amount of salt a vehicle has been exposed to in its past life. The weather

OPPOSITE
The Defender 90 commercial is a strong-selling vehicle countrywide

BELOW Whilst farmers are big users of Land Rovers, they never really took to them in the way the original designers envisaged

OPPOSITE Push the vehicle's attributes that suit the season in which you are selling or save money by buying out of season

is worse in the North, so more salt is spread on the roads there and older vehicles consequently tend to be in worse condition. Likewise exposure to salt air from the sea also speeds up corrosion. Vehicles used in London are exposed to less salt because the weather is warmer and less prone to icing. However, the motorway network is often heavily salted and vehicles driven on motorways are thus exposed to salt-laden spray, which tends to penetrate the vehicle structure and start corrosion.

With project vehicles it's harder to spot geographical variations. Down-at-heel vehicles, especially those with no MoT, tend to sell better away from the larger centres of population, in places where enthusiasts prepared to resurrect a vehicle with one wheel in the grave are more likely to be found. They also sell well to people prepared to break them up for spares and market the parts. Genuine historic vehicles will sell wherever they are, though, and travelling is all part of the buying experience for the enthusiast, who'll travel anywhere in the country or even the world to secure a rare, old, or elusive vehicle, the value of which is pretty constant wherever it's located. Less sought-after collectors' vehicles – such as 'just a Series I Land Rover' as opposed to 'a low chassis number 1948 Series I' – tend to be worth more, or at least find a new owner more readily, if they're located near the centre or south of the country, where enthusiasts with hobby money to spare are likely to be found. However, as demand increases and supply dwindles enthusiasts are becoming more prepared to get their trailer hitched up and go wherever the object of desire is located.

Seasonal variations

As well as geographical variations in value there are seasonal ones. These variations are partly in tune with the general motor trade economy: for example, Christmas and the arrival of credit card bills early in the New Year are enough to depress the market so that January, February, and March are difficult months in which to sell a vehicle. However, it's all forgotten when spring comes, and April, May, and June are buoyant months as people's thoughts turn to acquiring a new vehicle for the summer. Forget July and August, when holidays occupy everyone's attention. September, October, and November usually experience a bit of a revival, but come December car dealers are often better staying at home than wasting petrol travelling to the sales site.

Such variations affect demand and that in turn influences prices, especially the bottom value, which is the auction price. A canny dealer with money and space would stock up in January and February to sell on again a couple of months later but few do, instead paying more for exactly the same cars a few weeks later. Even on borrowed money the extra margin would be greater than the interest costs.

A shrewd purchaser will secure a better deal at a Land Rover dealer of any sort if he buys in the 'off season', especially during the winter months, as there are still overheads and expenses to pay and the dealer will try harder to get your custom. He'll also have more time to look after you and the buzz of a deal or the chance of reducing his overdraft a little will make him keener. Perhaps the best time of all to buy a vehicle from a dealer is the second week in January, when the post-Christmas depression is setting in and there's the prospect of a couple of lean months ahead. Selling a vehicle privately or at auction is more likely to be successful from the end of March onwards, when, even though it will have depreciated more, it's value may be less depressed than it would have been a couple of months previously.

There used to be a strong demand for 'banger' vehicles in December with enough MoT remaining to be used as a standby vehicle for bad weather. This was especially true in rural areas. However, there's no demand now because of the higher ownership of Freelanders and Discoveries by the sort of customer that might once have bought a standby. The high costs of ownership of an extra vehicle, the more ready availability of car-like 4x4 vehicles, and the seemingly milder winters have combined to kill off this seasonal market.

Soft-top vehicles also have a season and they're much harder to shift when it's cold and frosty. If you have a Freelander soft back with a hard top as well put that on for winter sales and offer the hood as an extra enticement in your advert; if the weather is hot and sunny do the opposite. Promote the aspect of your vehicle that's best suited to the season. Canvas tilt Land Rovers should be promoted the same way, though in reality a properly fitted tilt is often warmer and drier than a metal top. If buying, try to buy out of season when the price is lower, or use the fact that it's the wrong vehicle for the season as one of the bargaining points, even though it matters little, really, as most Land Rover products can be fitted with a hard back of some type at minimal expense.

Depreciation
and value

Depreciation

Depreciation is a word we've all heard, but what does it actually mean? The dictionary definition is devaluation, a drop or fall in something's monetary worth, and that's what's happening to the value of your car every second of its life.

It means that as a car gets older and more worn through use, people aren't prepared to pay as much to own it as they would be for a new one. It's quite a reasonable explanation really. It's usually expressed in a graph as value plotted against age or time, and the nearer to vertical the line is the greater the rate of depreciation, while a horizontal flat line represents nil depreciation. The shape of the curve, in mathematical terms, is a standard exponential decay curve.

The rate of depreciation can also be expressed as a percentage, usually over a year, referring to what remains of the money invested in a vehicle. Thus a 40 per cent depreciation rate in the first year means that for every £1,000 you invested in the vehicle only £600 would remain after the first year. This rate changes over the life of the vehicle and in terms of value retained it may make better financial sense to buy a second-hand expensive vehicle than a new cheaper one. It can therefore be argued that a three-year-old Range Rover is a better buy than a new Freelander for a similar price. It probably is if you look only at the vehicle value, but if you factor in all the other costs – such as maintenance of an older vehicle compared to a new one under warranty – the maths gets complicated and the outcome unpredictable. The choice between, for example, a Defender Station Wagon and a Discovery for the same money is much clearer, though. Although they have similar running costs, with its cheaper insurance and lower depreciation the Defender is the winner every time.

If you've bought a new Range Rover, for the first couple of years it sheds money just as if you had children on the back seat chucking a pound coin out of the window every mile. At 60mph on the motorway they'd probably not be able to chuck them out fast enough to keep up. £12K per year depreciation on a new Range Rover is about a pound a mile, or a pound a minute at 60mph! The rate of depreciation is highest in the first few minutes of a new car's ownership and slows down after about three to five years depending on model type. It slows again at ten years, and by twelve or so is almost a flat line, with value based on condition much more than age, and will continue flat for several years. If the vehicle deteriorates further it'll fall to a value slightly below the total sum of the value of the component parts. If the vehicle achieves true classic status it'll probably start to appreciate and rise in value again after reaching the age of about 18. The rate of depreciation is highest on Range Rovers, with the Discovery and Freelander about equal, and the Defender being the lowest by far.

Not all vehicles follow this traditional pattern, as some Land Rover products – such as the last of the Classic Range Rovers and some of the limited editions (the CSK and some of the Defender limited editions such as the 50, Heritage, and Tomb Raider, for example) – became classics in their own right long before their natural expected life time of 15 years was up and never decreased much in value after reaching six or seven years of age.

OPPOSITE
The Defender has always enjoyed the lowest rate of depreciation for any Land Rover product and special editions are even better

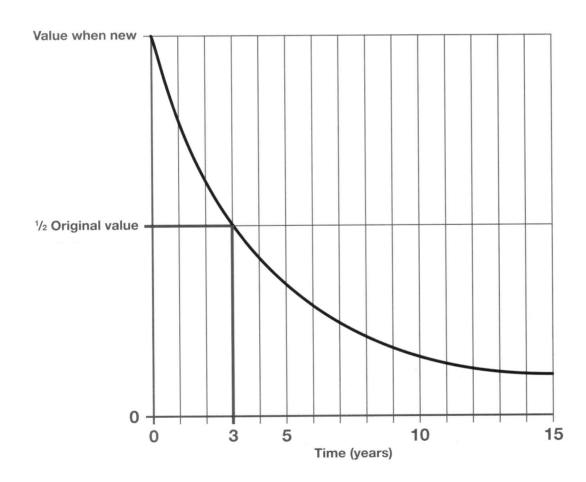

LEFT Typical Land Rover product depreciation curve

RIGHT The forecourt price is probably at least 30% greater than the true value of a vehicle

Value

The true value of a vehicle is the amount someone will give you for it as a straight deal in a reasonable time scale. This can be regarded as the base value for a vehicle, as it may have several other values that are usually higher. The first one is the perceived value in the mind of the owner. Human nature being what it is, we all want as much as possible for things, especially if we've spent some money on them. We also don't really like admitting that depreciation occurs, so we like to think our vehicle is worth almost what we paid for it. The owner's value, then, usually bears no resemblance to the actual value. However, the vendor might also value it too, especially with regard to older vehicles, and this may be to your advantage.

Book values are based on mathematical depreciation curves applied to the original cost of the vehicle, modified for condition and mileage. The actual shape of the mathematical model is dependent on the manufacturer, the type of vehicle, and loads of other parameters. Leasing costs are also based on these mathematical models, as they have to predict the value of a vehicle at two or three years of age, and as many vehicles are leased for the first years of their life the expected values and actual values are usually similar, or the motor trade wouldn't be able to function properly. The values plotted against age, then, have parallel curves for different sales situations such as a trade-in, forecourt price,

private sale, or trade sale. The difference between the trade and retail line is the dealer's mark up of about 20 per cent designed to cover a proportion of their site operating costs, bank charges, advertising costs, salaries, warranty expenses, business taxes, and VAT. Oh, and the free coffee that you have whilst sitting in the office deciding if you're going to buy or not. The trade sale is similar to the auction price and is really the true baseline value of a vehicle. The forecourt price is obviously highest, as it has to cover the overheads and profit margin of the business and allow a little for an exaggerated trade-in offer.

These standard depreciation curves (exponential decay curves) are applied by the specialists who write the books, and prices usually end up following the guides as they're the source that everyone is using, whereas one would expect the guide to follow the prices realised. Theoretically they're based on actual prices sampled from those that vehicles have sold for, but as these are following the guide it's difficult to work out if the prices make the guide or the guide makes the price. The authors of such things are a bit out of their depth with Land Rover products, especially so with Defenders. They're usually only found in the Commercial guides and are expected to follow the same sort of depreciation rate as a normal van. They depreciate much less than the guides might suggest and after a few years of age the guide is unrealistic. If you look at specific models such as the 110 Defender Station Wagon, for example, you'll find that it consistently fetches

LEFT The first of a
new model will always
fetch a premium over
the last of the old ones
of similar age

more than the guide price. In some cases they'll
make 120–160 per cent of the auction guide
price, whereas most other Land Rover products
(Freelander Discovery, Range Rover) achieve
about 93–97 per cent when sold at auction.

Land Rover products don't follow the standard
mathematically produced curves after the first
seven or eight years or so, and even though the
guide writers try to modify the prices, demand
means that Land Rovers fetch more money in a
retail sales situation than the guide would suggest
they're worth. This is especially true of popular
models. The guide is also optimistic with the
prices of models manufactured just before a
model change, as there's usually a bigger gap
than the guides might suggest between the last of
the Mk 2 Whatevers and the first of the Mk 3s, as
the market desirability of the new model forces its
price up and depresses the price of the last of the
old models. They can also be out on new models
on waiting lists, as in some exceptional cases a
three-month-old vehicle is worth more than it cost
new whereas the book has it at 80 per cent of its
cost price.

All the books – *CAP*, *Glass*, *Parker's*, or
whatever – have one common word on the front
cover, and that's 'Guide', which is exactly what
they are. A good way of valuing your vehicle is to
see what similar ones are fetching. Look on all the
websites, adverts, and auction result pages for
similar vehicles and add or subtract accordingly to
get a feel for the value of your vehicle. If similar
ones are up on forecourts for, say, £16,000 at a

main dealer and £15,000 at a specialist non-
franchised dealer, and they're making about
£12,000 at auction, then the true value of your
Land Rover in a private sale is probably an asking
price of £14,000, with a realistic likelihood of
getting £13,500.

A vehicle also loses value with a bump when
its ownership changes, whether it's a second-
hand vehicle or a new one. Using the example

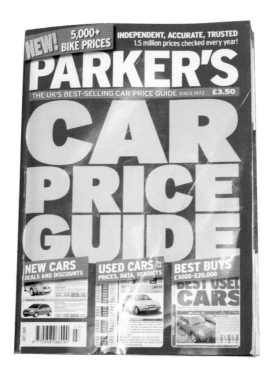

LEFT Readily available
books like this are a
great help when
valuing your Land
Rover, but remember
they are only a guide

RIGHT Replacing your
broken engine with a
new one will not add
to the vehicle's value
although it will add to
the desirability if there
is paperwork to back
the vendor's statement

above, if you bought the vehicle for £15,500 after
a bit of a haggle then it would only be worth
£12,000 after you've owned it for a couple of
days, as that's all you'd get for it if you suddenly
needed to sell it again. Whilst the dealer might
give you more than it was actually worth, they'd
only be doing so as a gentlemanly act of courtesy,
not as a straight commercial deal.

When valuing vehicles, owners naturally want
as much as possible and try to add the work
they've paid for to the value of the vehicle. Normal
routine servicing and maintenance doesn't add to
the value. It's only worth the figure it is because it
has the service history expected with newer
vehicles, while older vehicles need to have had
the work done to pass their MoT tests. As
regards breakages, the vehicle is worth no more
when it's repaired than it was a millisecond before
it broke: Range Rover value £10,000 + new
engine cost £5,000 = Range Rover value
£10,000, not the £15,000 that the unlucky owner
would like it to be.

Whilst having a new engine makes a vehicle
more desirable, and is a sales plus point, it adds
nothing to its value. Likewise clutches, gearboxes,
and other distress purchases or repairs add
nothing to the value. Normal routine replacement
of consumables such as tyres, exhausts, and
batteries are expected running costs, and such
items ought to be in good order for a vehicle to
maintain its expected value, especially in a private
sale environment. It's all too easy to put off a

buyer if the vehicle won't start for the sake of a
£30 battery. Likewise, a prospective purchaser will
be knocking off £600 in their head for a blowing
exhaust, not the £150 it would actually cost to fix
– that's if it doesn't put them off the vehicle
completely. Latent problems will also devalue your
vehicle when you try to trade it in, especially if the
dealer plans to retail it again. If it's a vehicle that
they'll trade out then it doesn't matter so much,
though obvious faults such as a blowing exhaust
would be better with a temporary repair to stop
them being obvious.

Almost any fault with a vehicle, from a blown-
up engine to a cracked headlight, will reduce the
value by significantly more money than it would
cost to fix. Similarly, dents and scratches on more
recent vehicles will devalue them a lot, as there's
a time factor as well as a money factor in having
them repaired. Obvious new paintwork can make
prospective purchasers wary of a vehicle as well.
After about ten years of age a few small blemishes
on the bodywork are par for the course, but
anything beyond fair wear and tear will still
devalue it.

The best way of valuing your vehicle, then, is to
see what similar vehicles are fetching in various
sales environments and then adjust the prices
according to the environment in particular and the
vehicles' condition (better or worse, higher or
lower mileage than yours), to reach a base figure
which will be similar to its auction value. The
actual average annual mileage is about 12,000
but the value correction figure is applied on the
basis of a standard annual mileage of 10,000.
Knowing this, work out how old the vehicle is and
deduct £20 from the base value for each
thousand miles above the annual mileage figure. In
theory you can add the same if it's below the
average figure, but unless it's extremely low for the
year then low mileage does little for the value.

A main dealer will typically add about 30 per
cent to this base price, a specialist about 20 per
cent, and a realistic private seller about 12.5 per
cent on his asking price, so multiply a dealer price
by 77 per cent, a specialist by 83 per cent, and a
private sale price by 88 per cent to get back to a
trade figure for a vehicle found in an advert, and
do it for as many examples as you can find of
similar specification and age to yours. Then
average them out, and what you end up with is
the value you'll probably be offered in a part
exchange deal. If selling privately, add about 12.5
per cent to get your asking price, and expect to
realise the base value plus about 10 per cent after
haggling.

These are the sorts of figures one expects with

vehicles retailing at a franchised main dealer at around the £15,000 level, but if the vehicle has £30,000 in its window on the forecourt the dealer's mark up will be a lot lower, probably about 15 per cent, as the expenses involved in retailing the vehicle will be about the same. If you find a vehicle at a specialist dealer for a £5,000 asking price then their mark up on the trade price may be as much as 40 per cent to cover the cost of preparation, etc. So the mark up or margin expressed as a percentage of the 'sticker price' is less for an expensive vehicle and more for a cheaper one. This is because it costs the same to advertise them, and the preparation costs and warranty costs are much higher with older vehicles, and it takes just as much time in terms of man-hours – or possibly even more – to sell a £2,500 vehicle as a £25,000 one. The only expense to cost less on a cheaper vehicle is the interest and other bank charges attributable to the vehicle if the dealer is using borrowed money.

These figures are a guide when selling or buying a vehicle, as you can't do either unless you have a realistic value. For example, you'll have great difficulty selling your Freelander from your drive for £16,500 if one exactly the same can be bought for £15,000 at a franchised main dealer. Likewise, if a specialist is retailing a Land Rover for £10,000 they're unlikely to offer £11,500 for a similar vehicle when you try to trade it in against something else.

It's unlikely that you'll undervalue your vehicle, as it's not human nature to do so. However, if by chance you mistakenly think it's only worth £5,000 and advertise it for this ridiculously low figure when specialist dealers are asking £10,000 the phone will possibly ring itself off the wall. On the other hand, it might not ring at all because people think there's something wrong with the vehicle.

Though a nice service record is desirable, you aren't paying for past history when you buy a vehicle. You're actually paying for its future life expectancy in terms of years of service and miles it can be driven before it has to be scrapped.

BELOW Almost all second hand Land Rovers are somewhere along the path to the scrapyard

Buying projects, ex-military, fleet and imports

Projects

Any vehicle that's not up to the standard one expects of it at a given age is worth much less than a good vehicle, and usually by much more than the cost of bringing it back up to standard if the work is done DIY.

One would normally expect more than four months' MoT left on a vehicle being offered for sale, so if you find one with only a week left, or even no MoT at all, and it needs money and/or time to get it through a test it can be to a purchaser's advantage to buy the vehicle more cheaply and employ their own time and skill to bring it up to scratch. This is especially true at the lower end of the market where every MoT is a bit of a lottery, but not at the top end where one might reasonably expect a properly maintained three-year-old vehicle to pass its first test without a problem.

This devaluation factor also applies to major mechanical problems such as blown-up engines, as well as less serious ones where the vehicle is still usable but isn't in the proper order that one might expect. Bodywork problems, from major accident damage to the gentle bruising found on many working Land Rovers (called 'farmer's wing'), have a similar effect on value. The purchaser can either repair the vehicle or live with the faults, knowing they saved money because of them. The problem, however, is how to value such vehicles.

With mechanical or MoT problems, don't take the vendor's word for what's required, as they often fail to remember something vitally important. Only take a recent MoT failure certificate as a reasonably accurate guide as to what's needed to get a vehicle back on the road. To restore it to a good standard often needs more work than the bare minimum required to pass a test. Likewise, 'Oh it just needs a head gasket' *might* be true, though it might actually need a new cylinder head or even a complete engine, as they can all present similar symptoms. So you need a 'win some, loose some' attitude when taking on a project, as well as the skill to ferret out replacement bits from salvage yards and internet sites so as to save money and make the project cost effective.

The sort of vehicles you can really save money on are lightly damaged insurance write-offs or tatty ex-farm vehicles that need a good clean and a couple of wings and seat cushions to get them back into order. Mechanical problems might include Discoveries with no drive because of gearbox failures, or Range Rovers that overheat because of engine failure. Insurance write-offs are registered on a database and will never achieve the value of an undamaged vehicle, as subsequent vendors should declare the fact to prospective purchasers, so they can't be regarded as a way of earning money by reselling them once they're repaired. If, however, you intend to use the vehicle yourself for a long time you'll have the satisfaction of knowing that it would have cost you several thousand pounds more to buy a better condition example from a dealer – if you could have afforded it at all.

Projects will always cost more to fix than the amount by which they're devalued if you include your time at the proper commercial rate, or have to pay someone else to do the work. So unless you have the necessary skill and facilities and more time than money they're best avoided.

The restoration of a classic Land Rover is a totally different sort of project, though, as they're usually appreciating assets and a lot of fun can be had from bringing them back from the edge. They usually cost more to do up than they're worth when first finished, but if you keep them for a year or two they steadily rise in value and you have the use of them as well. As a second or even third

vehicle the insurance is cheap, and since most were manufactured before 1973 they enjoy historic status and are free of road tax. There's also the opportunity of joining a local or national Land Rover club and spending leisure hours at shows and competitive or social events in the company of other people who own similar vehicles. It's a great sense of achievement as well, to drive a vehicle that's been brought back to life by your own hands.

It's a great thing to do, but never overestimate your skills or underestimate the time and money that's needed to complete a project. You need to be strong-willed to get it finished, and you'll find many vehicles being sold with the words 'abandoned project, much money spent' in their adverts. Some vehicles change hands several times in this state. Many fail to ever get back on the road and become increasingly beyond redemption before finally ending up as spares donors or scrap.

Only buy an historic restoration project if you realistically have the money, skill, time, devotion, and facilities, an understanding partner, and the resolution to see it through to completion. Before you do buy it, make certain that it's the vehicle it purports to be, that it's all there, that any work already done is to a proper standard, and that the price is realistic. Most people selling such abandoned projects will be losing money, and it gives you the opportunity to save some yourself – but only if you complete it. Never take on a 'second-hand' project without thoroughly inspecting it, as much of the previous work may well need to be done again if it hasn't been completed to a satisfactory standard in terms of either safety or historical accuracy. It's much easier to tackle 'virgin' rust than to sort out someone

BELOW Many projects take more money to complete than their end monetary worth, although this is not necessarily a reason not to do one as the pleasure of doing the work can be immense and be a profit in its own right

else's bodged repair attempt. Many inexperienced people also strip down vehicles and components to an unnecessarily great degree and then get overwhelmed by the enormity of the task facing them and eventually give up. If you have to sell a project on you'll also probably lose money if you don't finish it.

Classic vehicles are only worth money if they're restored to a condition similar to the original showroom state. Though much money may have been spent on preparing them for off-roading it will actually devalue a classic Land Rover or, if it was done a long time ago, will possibly stop it ever achieving its top value. It's a shame anyway to do this to an original old vehicle now, as there are many newer, cheaper, and better-suited vehicles to mess with. Unless they're of great historic importance it's unwise to buy ex-competition vehicles to restore, as the changes to their specification, welds on the chassis, and holes in the bodywork mean it's virtually impossible to achieve good results. With a classic restoration project you should ideally buy the best vehicle you can find that's least messed about and as complete as possible and to refurbish it, rather than take one totally to pieces and attempt to recondition it all.

The value of projects

Project vehicles of any type are one of the hardest things to value. In terms of repair or restoration costs deducted from the value of the finished item many vehicles would actually show a negative balance. As most vendors won't be giving you a wad of cash to take the vehicle away such projects need to be left alone or restored for the

love of it rather than in the hope of any commercial gain.

A project has three separate values that all combine to give its final value. Two are easy to ascertain. The third is much more difficult. And there's also a fourth potential value in some instances.

The first value is the sum of the component parts – the engine, gearbox, wheels, chassis, bodywork and so on – if stripped down and sold piecemeal, less the cost of disposing of the remains and the selling costs. Thus you can determine that an early diesel Discovery is worth £500–£1,000 because the sum of its parts is £1,500. A Series I Land Rover is worth about £300–£500, as most of the bits on it will be worn out and/or rusty and thus have little market value.

The second value is related to its potential to be used as a working vehicle again. With the tired Discovery in the previous paragraph this figure will be zero or close to it because the cost of repair will mean the project is worth the same as it cost or slightly less, so no value can be put on its potential. With the Series I this value will be from £300 to £1,500 or possibly even more, depending on what model it is and how rare it's considered to be by enthusiasts. With later vehicles suffering from body or mechanical damage this figure is based on their potential useful life expectancy and is therefore greater on newer vehicles.

Most project vehicles only have these two values, but some have two more. The third, on older vehicles and, indeed, more recent ones that have had 'cherished transfers', is the registration number value.

Though I don't condone the practice of stripping valuable registration numbers from old vehicles it's big business and they do have a value. This applies to original numbers still on old vehicles and to more recent numbers that have been bought and transferred to a vehicle. The first thing to do in all cases is to determine they still belong to the vehicle, that they're included in the sale, are that they're transferable. Then get them valued by a number plate dealer. The vehicle has to be taxed to get the number off and so needs a valid MoT test. It's all very well the vendor saying the number on an old rusty wreck is worth thousands but it's worthless if the vehicle can't be MoT tested, or at least stands a realistic prospect of being repaired sufficiently to test. Once you've included the cost of the transfer fee and new number plates, the devaluation (and loss of many potential customers) from a classic vehicle having a non-transferable reissued number, and the time

and effort spent taking the vehicle to a DVLA office for inspection, then unless the number is significantly valuable it's best left on the original vehicle. It really only adds value if the dealer considers it worth more than a thousand pounds. To ascertain a realistic valuation of a registration number multiply a dealer's offer by 75 per cent (as they don't usually achieve the original estimate) and knock off another £300 to cover transfer costs (DVLA fee, new number plates, and the trip to be inspected).

The fourth potential value is the 'Unique Selling Point' or USP, though this is even harder to value than the registration number. The USP can be defined as any factor that makes a vehicle so unique that a purchaser would have difficulty finding a similar one elsewhere. With Land Rover products this is often because they're Limited Editions. Heritage Defenders, Tomb Raider Defenders, Holland and Holland Range Rovers, and Millennium Discoveries are a few examples. They usually have a high specification and were limited to a batch of just a few hundred. Some editions, such as CSK Range Rovers and Defender V8 50s, have unique identifying numbers within the edition, such as a CSK 156/200 or GB261 on the Defender, usually stamped on a special metal plate fixed to the vehicle. These are even more sought after than the ordinary limited editions and so have an even higher USP value.

Another sort of USP results from a vehicle's past owners, whether pop stars, royalty, or famous footballers, so long as their ownership is documented. Ownership by the Rover Company, or more recently Land Rover, can also be a USP. Early prototypes and press launch vehicles are especially eagerly sought by enthusiasts and enjoy high USP values. Use in the Camel Trophy, G4, or other expeditions mean that even a battered and bruised vehicle is worth several thousand pounds more than a similar vehicle in better condition. However, there are many replicas of such vehicles so be very sure you're buying the real thing.

Most vehicles with a genuine history will have a file of information accompanying them. This will possibly include letters from the manufacturer or from BMIHT at Gaydon, period photographs, magazine articles, or information from a third party

to confirm the facts. It's not unknown for some vendors to be a bit fanciful in their ideas of a vehicle's previous life, so before paying for a Land Rover with an undocumented USP history check the facts with the owners' club relevant to that particular model (you needn't tell them where the vehicle's located) or by a phone call to BMIHT archives. The chassis number and possibly the registration number will confirm if the vehicle is genuine or not.

Most USP values can be ascertained by using similar vehicles as a guide and seeing how much more the asking price is than for a normal vehicle of the same age. Whilst strong sellers as collector or enthusiast vehicles when new, quite young limited editions such as the Heritage, Tomb Raider, and so on are currently still depreciating, though at a slower rate than other Land Rovers of a similar age. But as such vehicles get to the point where they start to appreciate – and this is at an earlier stage than normal vehicles of their type – the USP will appreciate too, and not necessarily at the same rate as the vehicle.

With truly unique vehicles the USP value is only what someone else is prepared to pay to own the vehicle, and advice from the relevant owners' club often helps to ascertain the correct value. Be wary of fakes as well – for example, there are quite a lot of fake Camel Trophy vehicles in circulation and not all of them are correctly described as replicas when being advertised. The appropriate club can advise you and authenticate the history of real vehicles. A USP isn't a tangible asset so be wary of overvaluation, especially by greedy vendors,

and be careful not to accept their valuation without doing some research yourself first.

It could be argued that historic vehicles are actually worth less than basic models, because to retain their historic status they need to be kept in original form and condition, which limits their future use and possibly enjoyment, as well as costing more money and time to own in maintenance terms. However, they're much sought after by collectors and enthusiasts so will always be worth more than a basic vehicle. Trigger words to be wary of in advertisements for such vehicles include 'rare' and 'collector's item', often misused to describe vehicles for which these terms aren't valid. Such words are usually a warning that the asking price may be over the top, with an unjustified USP value added in. If this is the case, don't be afraid to offer what you realistically think is a genuine price, even if it's only half or three-quarters of what's being asked, but be prepared for fireworks and at least have a sound, reasoned justification for your offer.

Ex-military, fleet and non-showroom vehicles

We now need to look at the pros and cons of ex-military and 'fleet' vehicles from bodies such as the police, electricity and water companies, the Environment Agency, the AA and the RAC, as well as non-'showroom specification' vehicles.

OPPOSITE
Although most purchasers would usually avoid a battered vehicle, if they are genuine scars from this sort of use then they actually add to the USP and hence the value

LEFT This is a unique Land Rover factory concept vehicle called the Olympic and its USP value is several times greater than its value simply as a 20-year-old Range Rover

Land Rover products have, by their very nature, always been bought in large quantities by the military, the police, utility companies and the like. At the end of a fixed time period, or when a target mileage has been reached, these are invariably disposed of. Sometimes, if the target mileage hasn't quite been reached and an expensive repair presents itself, they're sold on as non-runners. In general they're well looked after and replacement components and tyres are usually of good quality. They're often the only source of second-hand vehicles of some types. Defender 130s and Crew Cabs, for example, are bought new almost exclusively by commercial users.

Such vehicles may not be to showroom specification. They may just be a different colour, such as AA yellow or NATO green, or they may have different seating configurations, extra batteries, heavy-duty suspension, heaters and winches. Often the cost of such extras would have doubled the price of the vehicle when new. In some cases even the engine isn't the same as in the ordinary civilian type.

The military clung on to the 2.5 normally aspirated diesel engine and then the 300TDI long after normal production vehicles had moved on to turbochargers and TD5 engines. Military vehicles often have different wiring and lighting configurations. They also tend to have sliding windows rather than the wind-up type and manual rather than power-assisted steering. It has been said that military Land Rovers were built up to a specification whereas civilian ones were built down to a price, but even though that's possibly true it's not a good reason to buy one, as the specification

may have been for 24v electrics and other complications that a civilian user won't need. Finally, they usually have several coats of matt green and black paint applied by brush and require a lot of effort to be restored to a shiny civilian finish. But having said all that, military vehicles fetch a premium price when first released and continue to do so for the rest of their civilian lives.

In general fleet Land Rovers have endured a hard life and aren't the tidiest of vehicles externally when sold, but they've usually been well looked after. Their usage has often been better as well. With most wear occurring during the first few miles of driving, when the engine isn't at operating temperature, 250 miles clocked up on a single shift will cause considerably less wear to a police Range Rover than to a similar vehicle doing the same mileage in a hundred return trips to school.

Fleet vehicles are usually expensive to refurbish to a high standard, as it's expensive to sort out the interior and the bruised bodywork. They're usually high mileage for their age and often not in popular colours. High motorway mileage and use in extreme weather often means that ex-emergency service and utility company vehicles have had a high exposure to road salt, so that even though quite young a vehicle may be starting to corrode quite badly.

On the other hand they've invariably been well maintained, are usually high specification, and they retain many of their extras when sold on. They usually represent value for money – except for ex-military vehicles, which as already mentioned fetch premium prices. In the past this was because military vehicles were little used and often stood in store for years. In the modern world this is no longer true, however, as the use of individual vehicles is now much higher and many will have seen hard service in wars and peacekeeping roles. You therefore need to be very sure before buying one that you can't find a better version for less money elsewhere.

For reasons of simplicity and accounting transparency most fleet vehicles are initially sold off at auction or sometimes by tender, often in batches, and then refurbished and retailed by the specialist independent Land Rover trade. Often this will involve repainting in a standard Land Rover colour and fitting seats and windows, etc, to bring them up to a recognisable specification. There's nothing to stop an individual buying one and doing the work themselves, and the specialist 4x4 auctions would be a good place to start looking.

Imported vehicles

For several years now it's been possible to buy new right-hand-drive Land Rovers from a Continental dealer and to import them back into this country at a price-saving for the end user. Several businesses have set up in the UK specialising in selling new Land Rovers for a few thousand pounds less than your local main dealer. A lot also end up for sale at the car supermarkets. There's no way of distinguishing the origin of a vehicle from its registration document, as if it was imported new the date of registration in the UK and first use are the same, though the service book usually has the Continental dealer's stamp on the first page. With the advent of pan-European warranties all work can be done at a local dealer, so there are no problems getting things fixed under warranty. However, franchised dealers can tell from their computer system where a vehicle came from, and they don't value them as highly as identical UK models if you try to trade one in. If auctioned, however, a vehicle's foreign origin usually doesn't show up, the service book being missing entirely or having its first page missing or a sticker over the supplying dealer, and it probably won't be declared as having been imported.

When new such vehicles were 10–20 per cent below list price and ought to be regarded as that sort of percentage less in value throughout their life. In practice, though, as the prices fall and they're no longer in main dealer sales territory, the value of imported and UK-sourced vehicles becomes the same at about six or seven years of age, when overall condition starts to have a bigger impact on value than theoretical depreciation.

Other vehicles that have been used and registered abroad may have belonged to, for example, someone owning a Continental property or serving in the armed services. The vehicles may be left-hand-drive or even have been converted to right-hand-drive. Registered using an age-related number in the UK, the registration document will say they're imported and used previously abroad. There's no problem buying one of these, as it's likely to be an older vehicle and possibly in a less rusted condition than a home-market one. Price really reflects condition and there ought to be no negative penalty for the paperwork.

There are also numerous Discoveries and Range Rovers being returned from Japan, where they were bought as status symbols but after ten years or so are worth more in this country as their status has dropped on account of age. They're usually low mileage and corrosion free when sold and, of course, are right-hand-drive, meaning that they're excellent buys, though at a price premium. As a longer term investment, say three years and over, this is fine, but if you wanted to sell one on again in the shorter term it would be difficult to get back the extra premium that you paid compared to a UK-sourced vehicle, despite its better bodywork.

Some ex-military vehicles may show up as imported on their V5C, especially ones that were released a few years ago. This is nothing to worry about – it just means they were initially disposed of wherever they were in use, such as in Germany or Cyprus, and were brought back to this country by the dealer before resale.

ABOVE The MOD has run the biggest single UK fleet of Land Rovers for the last fifty years and have them built to their own unique specifications and paint finishes

Knowing your rights

When you sell or buy a vehicle the nature of the deal will determine what legal protection is available, if any at all, if you're unfortunate enough to encounter a problem. A dealer obviously has to provide a great deal more than a private individual, which is why at the lower end of the dealer spectrum many try to pass themselves off as private individuals in an effort to absolve themselves of their legal responsibilities.

The main legal responsibility that applies to both new and second-hand vehicles sold by a motor trader is that they aren't inherently faulty, and that's the liability such people are trying to escape from. You actually pay for this protection in the price, which is one of the reasons why a private sale price needs to be lower than a dealer's.

Buying from a dealer

Anyone buying from an outlet operating as a retail motor dealer, whether Land Rover franchised or not, is covered by the 1979 Sale of Goods Act (see Appendix 5), which basically means that the Land Rover being sold has to be of merchantable quality and fit for the purpose for which you're buying it. It doesn't mean it has to be like new, but it has to be in the sort of order one might reasonably expect from a vehicle of that price, age, and mileage. It ought to be free of latent faults, but if there's a problem and it's not resolved to your satisfaction you can, in theory, reject it within a reasonable time – which with a vehicle is really within the first two weeks. In practice it's difficult to do this, especially if it wasn't a latent fault and the dealer does his best to sort it out for you. If you've bought the vehicle on a finance agreement you can reject it with the finance company, which in law actually owns the vehicle. If you do reject it send letters to the dealer by recorded delivery, and it may be worthwhile consulting a lawyer, both for advice and to make it more official.

If there's a problem with a new Land Rover it's legally the supplying dealer's responsibility to sort it out, as your contract is with them and not the manufacturer, though they'll ultimately foot the bill.

Buying privately

You have no protection buying privately unless the vendor doesn't have clear title to the vehicle or doesn't tell the truth. If you find it's still on finance or not theirs to sell, or they told you it hadn't been an insurance write-off when asked and you subsequently found out that it was, or they lied in the description, especially about the mileage, then you have a comeback and the Trading Standards office or possibly even the police (if an offence such as theft, fraud, deception or similar has been committed) will possibly take the matter up for you.

Unfortunately the burden of proof means that false statements about mileage etc need to have been in the advert, or to appear on the receipt for the sale, to be worth investigating. A verbal statement is impossible to prove or disprove, so get important details such as mileage written into the receipt. The vendor has no legal obligation to disclose anything to you about the vehicle, such as previous accident damage, but if asked should answer truthfully and to the best of their knowledge.

If there's a mechanical or other physical problem with the vehicle that you were not aware of and you discover it soon after taking delivery then unfortunately it's your problem. *Caveat emptor*, meaning 'buyer beware', is the phrase you need to constantly repeat to yourself when buying privately. In law you may possibly be in the right when it comes to resolving issues with a private purchase if a problem subsequently comes

to light, but in practice it's usually very difficult and expensive to get satisfaction. It's even more difficult to resolve if it's a readily available fact that might have shown up on a database enquiry before buying the vehicle.

Buying at auction

If you buy from a regulated auction you have a guarantee of good title and usually pay an indemnity fee to cover yourself as a purchaser in the unlikely event that the vehicle shouldn't have been sold. With the nature of trading it's very common not to have the vendor's name in the paperwork and the system is open to fraud, though

ABOVE Buying privately gives no protection from a hidden history

BELOW If it all falls apart on the way home, you have no recourse in a private or auction sale

this is rare. The indemnity fee is an insurance to cover you if the deal is subsequently found to be fraudulent, as you're not actually buying from the auction house, which is merely acting as an agent for the entrant, so that in law you have no claim against them in the unlikely event of a problem.

Vehicles are sold in one of two ways: warranted and unwarranted. In the first instance the vehicle is declared free from major mechanical defects or such faults are listed, so that if you discover a mechanical problem that you could not reasonably see on inspection you can return the vehicle for a refund, usually within an hour of the sale ending. Unwarranted means there's absolutely no comeback whatsoever.

Buying on the internet

There are now great money-saving opportunities to buy from traders who source UK spec vehicles abroad and, because of exchange rate vagaries and the pricing structures in different countries, can sell them to you for less than your local Land Rover Dealer and yet still make a living. Sometimes they buy within the UK but operate with lower overheads than franchised dealers and can consequently sell for less money. You're covered by the 1979 Sale of Goods Act. If you didn't physically visit the vendor's premises and bought over the internet or telephone you also have a seven day cooling-off period in which to cancel the contract and return the vehicle.

Buying abroad

If you buy a vehicle from a dealer abroad, whether to import yourself or to keep in another country, the laws applied are those of the country of purchase and you have no recourse in UK law, though most EU countries operate similar rules. With pan-European warranties any work can be carried out in the UK or wherever the vehicle is located without having to return it to the supplier, even though the original sale contract was with them. If, however, there was some insurmountable problem and you felt you needed to reject the vehicle the action would be against the supplier in their country under their law and would probably be complicated by the fact that you aren't a national. Fortunately, the instances where a Land Rover product needs to be rejected are few and far between so this can be regarded as a minimal risk.

Buying in an internet auction

You have the protection of the auction provider but usually that's limited to items sold for less than £500. If their dispute resolution fails you have the protection applicable to a private or trade purchase as appropriate to the declared status of the vendor in the listing. In practice it will be very difficult to sort out a problem, so treat an internet auction as if you have absolutely no protection from anything. Before paying for the Land Rover check it out on the DVLA website and do a status check, and proceed with caution. In the private sector, remember, it's buyer beware, so don't expose yourself to situations where you might need protection, such as paying for the vehicle before taking delivery. As vendors won't release a vehicle until they have the money paying cash may be appropriate.

Warranties

Warranties only apply to new vehicles for a period of three years, and possibly to second-hand ones sold by a trader. The circumstances of the sale determine the legal warranty and the service offered by the vendor over and above this.

Land Rover provides a full three-years parts and labour unlimited mileage guarantee on its new vehicles and this stays with the vehicle even if it changes hands. It basically covers everything except wear and abuse though there are certain criteria to be fulfilled, such as servicing at the proper intervals though not necessarily at the supplying main dealer. If you buy privately you'll inherit the balance of the three years provided nothing has been done in the past to jeopardise your right to having the work done. The terms and conditions of the warranty are available from a dealer.

Land Rover is also good at contributing towards known problems that become apparent just outside the warranty period. Though not obliged to, if asked they'll consider each case on its merits and pay or contribute as they see fit.

If you buy second-hand from a main dealer, in addition to any remaining manufacturer's warranty or legal obligation they'll probably give a full 12 months' parts and labour warranty of their own on any vehicle they sell retail. This also usually has terms and conditions, such as having it serviced with them, though these vary between dealers.

This is obviously an expense for them and explains why vehicles cost more from such a source.

If you buy from another trade source as a retail deal they'll probably include or sell you a warranty insurance that lasts for 12 months. This is a bought-in warranty insurance and it isn't the responsibility of the vendor to sort out problems after an initial period. The dealer is usually responsible for the first month and the warranty company for rest of the time. On the face of it such warranties look like good value, but they only cover breakages and not failure from use or wear. In some cases they also require contributions from the owner towards 'betterment' and for consumables such as oil and filters. You also need a repair to be approved before work can start. So though they sound like good value they're usually less good when you read the small print or try to claim. They also often have a ceiling on the repair costs or a limit to the number of claims. Though true, 'Full 12 month warranty' on a windscreen sticker as an enticement to buy might not have quite the meaning you perceive when it comes time to call on it.

Some independent dealers give their own 'proper' warranties for varying lengths of time after sale, and though you hopefully don't need to utilise them their inclusion or lack of it must be considered in any deal. Check its parts and labour coverage, as some may be parts-only.

Though you may have to push them to admit it traders are legally obliged to sort out problems for a reasonable length of time after purchase and this can be taken as about a month, as within this period it's highly likely that the fault was present when you bought the vehicle. If they're reluctant just start muttering phrases such as 'merchantable quality' or 'fit for the purpose'. They're not obliged to sort out problems that have occurred since purchase, though most are reasonable people and will usually 'stand by their vehicles for a month', as they want to retain their reputation and your custom. They tend not to like being pushed, bullied, or accused of knowingly selling a duff vehicle, so the grown-up and polite approach is best rather than the ranting and raving that often happens when an owner is upset. Self-made problems through accident or abuse are understandably not covered by anyone on any age of vehicle from any source.

So ask for the exact terms of a warranty if one is on offer. Make certain it's a written statement, not verbal, so that it's plain to see who's responsible for what and can't be misunderstood. Spend time with the small print. Read the terms and conditions before you make your mind up

LEFT A manufacturer approved vehicle with franchised dealer full warranty is the best warranty you can get

whether to buy a vehicle from this vendor or from another. Warranties aren't all-inclusive and don't usually cover things you've damaged yourself or consumables such as tyres, bulbs, and so on that you'd normally have to replace periodically anyhow.

In an auction 'warranty' has a different meaning. It's not a guarantee to fix the vehicle if it breaks, but an assurance that there are no undeclared major mechanical problems with it. This means you don't have to check for clutch slip or knocking big ends before you bid, as you don't get the opportunity to drive the vehicle. It means you're assured that there are no problems and if you find them when you've paid for the vehicle it can be returned for a full refund within 24 hours or sometimes within just an hour from the end of the sale.

In a private sale there's no guarantee whatsoever, so once you've paid and the vehicle is yours so too is the responsibility for repairing any faults, whether they were present before purchase or if they appear later. The lower price you should have paid is partly to cover the risk of repair costs.

BELOW Some used vehicles on sale still carry the balance of the manufacturer's three-year warranty as well as the dealer's own

Financial
matters

Finding the money

Because of their high value most recent and new Land Rovers will be purchased initially through some sort of finance scheme. We don't all have the funds readily available to buy a vehicle and even if we did, income tax benefits, especially for business owners and users, sometimes mean it's preferable to fund the vehicle another way.

Your personal credit history is examined before anyone will lend you money or lease a vehicle to you, so you need to make certain it's in order, as a refusal is most embarrassing. Check what's on your record through Experian or Equifax (see Appendix 1) and amend anything that may be incorrect or missing, such as your inclusion on the Electoral Roll at your current address, and may be adversely affecting your credit rating. You'll also be credit scored, which is a look at your current commitments and ability to repay the loan. You may have a perfect history, but if they see too many obligations for too little income the lender won't award you enough points and the loan will be refused. The scoring is based on information you put down on the loan application form and details of existing loans and mortgages listed with the credit reference agencies.

Cash

Cash, as opposed to credit in this context and not actual folding money, is the preferred method of finding the funds to pay for a vehicle, though in reality as the figures increase less and less of us have the amount needed to fund a vehicle readily available. Even if you're lucky enough to have the money it doesn't always get you the best deal, as not all dealers want you to pay for a vehicle, as this deprives them of a sizeable commission cheque from the finance company with whom you sign up. It's a quick deal for them, though, and takes less of their time, so swift payment will help though don't expect a cash discount just because you're paying for the vehicle directly.

Bank loan

Borrowing from a bank or other financial institution has got to be the next best way of raising the money. Most will lend you the money, which is placed in your account so you can treat it as cash when you buy a car. You can therefore buy from a private vendor or at auction as well as from dealers, as you have quick access to the funds. You don't need to find a deposit from your own money as you can just borrow the full amount. The long time periods over which the loan can be repaid may seem attractive, and with Land Rover products lasting longer than most cars it's attractive to use them, but if you borrow over seven years (which is usually the maximum) the vehicle could be well worn by the end of that time and you'll still be paying for a vehicle that's long gone.

It's often expensive to borrow small amounts and it may be cheaper in the long run to buy a more expensive vehicle that will last you for longer, as the interest rates reduce the more you borrow. A loan is easy to arrange before you go out to buy a vehicle, and you can therefore separate the two procedures and so pay due attention to both of them. Lenders often try to sell you a payment protection plan to cover the monthly payments if you fall ill or become unemployed. However, these are expensive and you need to read the small print very carefully as the protection may not be suitable for you. Comprehensive insurance is advisable though not compulsory. You own the vehicle from the start, which is an advantage, but some lenders will want to use your house as security for the loan, especially if the amount borrowed is quite high. If the loan needs to be secured then it's much cheaper in monthly repayment terms to extend your mortgage.

Hire purchase

This is a loan from a finance company in which you put down an initial deposit and the balance has to be repaid in equal monthly instalments, usually 24 or 36 though terms of up to five years are possible. The vehicle is yours at the end of the payments though you don't own it until the very last payment has been made. A hire purchase agreement is easy to arrange if your credit record is OK. It's not too expensive, but if you have a poor record the charges are astronomical, if indeed you're even accepted. Comprehensive insurance is compulsory, as the owners want their asset covered against damage and theft. As you don't own the vehicle it's thought to be easier to reject it if it's a dud, though in practice this is difficult. The supplying dealer will do his best to sort it out, though.

Because the dealer needs a Consumer Credit licence you're limited to buying from a registered trader who will usually only use the finance company he's registered with, so you can't shop around for a better interest rate. The dealer will often add spurious amounts to the agreement, such as a purchase fee or administration fee, which you ought not to pay as they're already on commission. You need a deposit either in ready funds or in the residual value of a trade-in, and as well as the high interest rates there's an early settlement fee if you need to sell the vehicle before the period is up. As most agreements are over relatively short periods of two or three years the monthly repayment figure is quite high. If your current vehicle is on finance it's often possible for the dealer to settle this and provide you with another vehicle without you having to find any extra money, though the new agreement may involve higher instalments for a longer period.

As interest rates go it's quite an expensive way of borrowing for a vehicle. Independent companies don't have as strict lending or vehicle criteria as the manufacturer but it's difficult to get finance on anything over five years of age and almost impossible if it's over seven, and if you do it will be for a short period of probably 24 months. Some dealers can get pre-approval for you before you decide what vehicle to buy, which will help you decide beforehand rather than get disappointed when you set your heart on something beyond the reach of your pocket.

Lease/personal contract plan

Businesses can lease vehicles, which in effect means renting them over a long period. Numerous lease companies offer these schemes and they supply the vehicle directly to your premises. Leases are usually only available on new or very young vehicles.

18 August 2004

Dear

We are pleased to supply details of the Land Rover Freedom terms currently available through Land Rover Financial Services, subject to status. These terms are effective on the above date only as finance quotations may be subject to change. If you wish to proceed, please contact us so that arrangements can be made to complete a credit application.

Vehicle: LAND ROVER DEFENDER 90 XS STATION WAGON

Registration Number (if known) : **Engine : 2.5 TD5**

Mileage Per Annum : 21000		Excess Charges : 10p per mile + VAT					
On the Road Cash Price :					£	23850.00	
Less Advance Payment :			£	4000.00			
			£	4000.00	£	4000.00	(A)
Amount of Credit					£	19850.00	
Total Charge for Credit:	Interest		£	5647.68			
	Facility Fee		£	105.00			
(Payable with GFV)	Purchase Fee		£	75.00	£	5827.68	
Balance payable (incl. Optional Final Purchase Payment)					£	25677.68	(B)
Optional Final Purchase Payment (Guaranteed Future Value)					£	6881.00	
Representing a Total Amount Payable of (A+B)					£	29677.68	
Payable by 36 monthly installments of					£	**517.13**	

Total Monthly Payment	£	**517.13**
APR		**14.7%**

Total charge for credit includes a finance facility fee of £105 (where applicable) payable with the First Instalment and a £75 purchase fee that will be collected with the Guaranteed Future Value.

Payment Protection cover may be available. We strongly recommend that you protect your payments. Please ask for a Payment Protection policy booklet for full details of benefits and exclusions.

Under the agreement you will be required to keep in force a comprehensive motor insurance policy in respect of the goods, with an insurer of your choice.

At the end of the agreement you have three options:

1. You can trade the vehicle in to the supplying dealer and pay the Optional Final Purchase Payment, using any money over this amount as deposit towards a new vehicle. Alternatively, the vehicle can be sold privately and you can keep the profit over the Optional Final Purchase Payment, which must be paid to Land Rover Financial Services. You gain the benefit of any value in excess of the Optional Final Purchase Payment (you must tell Land Rover Financial Services before you sell the vehicle as it belongs to Land Rover Financial Services until you have made all your payments under the agreement.

2. If the vehicle is worth less than the Optional Final Purchase Payment, you can return the vehicle to Land Rover Financial Services. Provided that you return the vehicle in reasonable condition and your agreed mileage has not been exceeded, you will have nothing further to pay.

3. You may purchase the vehicle at the Optional Final Purchase Payment, detailed on the previous page.

Please do not hesitate to contact us at the address above should you have any questions.

Yours sincerely

The same sorts of scheme are offered to individuals and are called personal contract hire. Usually all the fixed costs such as tax, insurance, servicing and tyres are covered and all you do is put in fuel. There's usually a big cash deposit needed as part of the payment and you hand the vehicle back after 24 or 36 months. You can buy it at the end of the period for a single payment sometimes called a 'balloon payment', the amount of which is known from the start. Also referred to as the 'future resale value' or something similar, this is often less than the true market value. The monthly payment figures, though, are quite small.

Leasing is a good option in some regards, as it's a fixed budget figure and cash flow forecasting is easy, and it's also tax efficient for companies as the vehicle isn't an asset. But for a private individual it's an expensive way of funding a vehicle. There are also strict terms imposed, and mileage higher than the agreed figure of, usually, 12,000 miles per year is charged to you at quite high rates. There are also penalties for scratches and body damage and anything above fair wear and tear.

Manufacturer or main dealer finance

Franchised dealers also offer finance, both for new vehicles and for suitably approved second-hand ones, through Land Rover Financial Services, a trading name of FCE Bank plc. FCE is short for

Ford Credit Europe and is wholly owned by Ford Credit International Inc, which in turn is owned by the Ford Motor Company, the owner of Land Rover.

The most common route is the PCP (Personal Contract Purchase). The interest rates can be expensive but at the end of the term you can buy the vehicle for a fixed price and hand it back or trade it in, using any surplus between the trade-in figure and the Optional Final Payment figure as part of the deposit on your next vehicle. You can also sell it privately and keep any excess after making the Final Payment to the lender. The final figure you need to pay is usually quite a lot lower than the vehicle's market value, so even if the payments are expensive you can sometimes recover some of the expense this way, but you either need the funding to be able to purchase it or else you need to sell it on swiftly with the lender's permission. The actual monthly payment figures are based on the amount of deposit that you put down (0–35 per cent), the predicted annual mileage, and the length of term.

Hire purchase is also offered through Land Rover Financial Services for both new and used vehicles, with varying term lengths and rates. This too is provided through FCE Bank plc. The vehicle becomes your property at the end of the term, either to continue to use, to sell, or to use as a deposit on your next Land Rover, but unless you put down a sizeable deposit the monthly repayments can be quite high. The manufacturer's criteria for both age

LEFT
The manufacturer offers several schemes of acquiring a new vehicle through its current owner, the Ford Motor Company

short-term method if you're getting funds from elsewhere to pay the card off after a few weeks. It limits you to trading at a dealer who takes cards and there'll usually be a surcharge of 2.5 per cent or even more, which is the commission they have to pay the card company. Some people take advantage of 0 per cent balance transfers and change card issuer every six months in order to get an interest-free loan. However, you need to be really disciplined to do this as if you get it wrong the interest will be horrific.

Credit cards can be utilised as a means of short-term finance whilst you sell your other vehicle to repay the debt, or as a way of paying at auction immediately, thereby giving you the time to release funds from elsewhere, but they should never be used for the long-term financing of anything.

Equity release

The cheapest way to borrow money is to take advantage of the rise in value of your house and to extend the mortgage or take out a loan against it. Whilst this is cheap in terms of repayment figures per month you'll in effect still be paying for a vehicle several years after it's gone. On the other hand you can regard the rise in value of your house as a bit of a windfall and spend it on a car and so be paying for the house at its current worth over the longer term, which is really what you're doing.

ABOVE Debit cards are the perfect way to pay for a Land Rover, but Credit cards are a poor way to fund one

and condition of vehicle are quite strict and they need to be convinced of your ability to keep up the payments. Even though it adds to your outgoings it may be a good idea to look at GAP (Guaranteed Automobile Protection) insurance.

Credit cards

These should be avoided as a long-term way of raising funds for a vehicle, as the interest they rack up is very high. However, they may be a good

RIGHT Whilst equity release may seem a good plan to fund a Land Rover, you might still be paying for it long after it has gone

Equity release is a good way of financing your purchase if you can afford the extra repayments, though if interest rates rise in the future it may not look so attractive several years down the line. It has the advantage of enabling you to raise a quite large sum of money easily and use it as cash so that you're free to buy wherever you want. The disadvantage is that the Land Rover will be dropping in value all this time so your personal net worth will be reducing.

General

When you're borrowing money pay special attention when the time comes for the bank or dealer to run through the paperwork. If you can manage it, separate the process of buying the vehicle from the money-raising process, as if you're still thinking about the vehicle you're prey for an unscrupulous dealer to rip you off. Watch the annual percentage rate, as this is the best way to judge the merits of one offer against another. Changes in the APR may be quite small but represent a significant difference in the monthly payments. A difference of just 0.1 per cent in the APR is about £20 per month over three years so if they quote a figure be sure the documentation is the same and not just close to it. Be wary of fees added in, such as purchase fee and facility fee, and if you're offered payment protection make certain you can't get cheaper cover elsewhere. Also check the length of time the agreement is for, the shorter the better as long as the payment is achievable.

Be certain in your mind what it is you're signing up to. Is it personal contract hire where you pay to use the vehicle and give it back at the end, or is it hire purchase where it's all yours once the final payment is made? In fact I strongly advise you to take time out between the buying bit and the finance side if you're doing both at the dealer, so that you can take off your car buying head and put on your money borrowing head. Even if it's just a walk round the block it will help to clear your mind so that you can pay proper heed to the money aspects.

It's usually a buyers' market, with there being plenty of stock on offer at dealers, so even though you may fall for a certain vehicle another dealer may have its twin sister in stock and might do you a better deal on the vehicle and/or the finance package. It will pay you to shop around and to play one dealer off against another to get the best deal and the best interest rates possible, remembering that the slightest difference in the APR is a significant amount of change in the monthly repayments.

Payment protection plans and GAP insurance

If you buy a vehicle on some sort of finance arrangement everything's fine so long as you can make the repayments, but if you're suddenly unable to pay through no fault of your own it can be quite stressful. If you lose your job or are unable to work due to illness it's possible you may be covered if you had the foresight to take out payment protection insurance when you signed the agreement. Most lenders will offer a payment protection plan with the loan but it's often quite expensive. A decent insurance broker will usually be able to arrange better cover for less money and may even be able to arrange decreasing cover in line with the decreases in the outstanding balance of the loan as time progresses. Get quotations from other sources before you sign with the lender so that you can compare costs.

Most finance companies and banks will try to persuade you to take up their own brand of payment protection insurance. You might think they have your interests at heart but in fact it's just their profits they're looking after, as it's a very lucrative sort of insurance. The cost is about 10 per cent of the borrowed figure, and as it's payable in advance it's added to the balance and you consequently pay interest on it too so that it adds between 12 and 25 per cent to the monthly figure depending on term length. Thus a £500 repayment becomes £560. If you borrowed £15,000 at an APR of 7.2 per cent over seven years, which is an average sort of personal loan, the payments would be £227 without insurance and £304 with, meaning that over the term it costs £77 a month for the PPI. This is an extra £6,468 over the period, or £924 a year.

The insurance companies are often reluctant to pay out when it comes to it and even when they do it's usually only for 12 months. So if it's a long-term problem and a long finance period you'll be in trouble after 12 months. We all tend to burden ourselves with too much debt and this extra bit may be the last straw. Personally I'd suggest not taking up the PPI option and would advise you to look elsewhere for the insurance or to do it DIY by paying an equivalent sum of money into a separate account each month. Taking the example described in the previous paragraph, if you did this DIY you'd be four payments in hand after the first year and after three years would have all of the 12 payments in hand that the insurance would probably pay out. However, you do need strict self-discipline to do it this way.

The PPI won't usually pay out for self-employed people either, though they might take your money and call it a mistake if you were unlucky enough to claim. If you are self-employed or are careful with money, instead of using the PPI take out a personal accident and sickness insurance through an insurance broker to cover the monthly payments and a life cover for the loan. This can be a decreasing cover insurance, as it's cheaper to take out since you need less cover as the term progresses, with the outstanding balance decreasing as you pay the borrowed money back.

Sometimes, though, the interest rates quoted are higher if you don't take out the PPI, as it's perceived that there's a greater risk of not getting paid if it all goes wrong, so watch that the rates don't rise between quote and acceptance.

There's another situation in which you may need extra insurance and that's if your Land Rover gets damaged or stolen and its value for insurance purposes – and thus the amount the insurer will be prepared to pay out on it – is less than the outstanding finance. Your cover won't extend to the finance charges that have been added to the cost of the vehicle and even with an early settlement rebate you'll usually owe more than the vehicle is worth, especially in the first half of the repayment period. The insurance company, in the event of a claim, will only offer you the market value, which is similar to the trade-in value. It's possible to take out GAP insurance for a relatively small sum, which will cover the difference in the event of a total loss claim. The GAP decreases as time progresses but can sometimes be as much as £10,000 or even more on a recent Land Rover, so insurance cover is well worth considering.

APR

APR stands for the annual percentage rate of charge and can be used to compare different credit and loan offers. The APR is the equivalent interest rate after taking into consideration all the additional costs of taking out a loan. Naturally, it's a function of the loan amount, the interest rate, the total added cost, and the length of term. The APR would equal the interest rate only if there's no additional cost to a given loan, but as it includes the charges for documentation and so on it's greater than the actual percentage rate. Sometimes these charges are listed separately to the loan to lower the quoted APR figure. When comparing loans you must judge them as like for like and this is the function of the APR. So check whether or not they all include the charges before comparing them.

As the APR takes into account not just the interest on a loan but also the other charges you have to pay – for example, any arrangement fee – all lenders have to tell you what their APR is before you sign an agreement. It will vary from lender to lender. Generally, the lower the APR the better the deal for you, so if you're thinking about borrowing, shop around. Don't forget that sometimes bank loans are cheaper than the credit schemes offered by dealers. If you find a deal with a low APR, ask the following questions:

1. Does the interest included in the APR vary, or is the rate fixed? If the rate is variable, your repayments could go up or go down. If the rate is fixed, your repayments will stay the same.

2. Are there any charges that aren't included in the APR? This could include something like optional payment protection insurance. If so, make sure you understand what they are and when you'd have to pay them, and see if you can find the same cover for less elsewhere.

3. What are the conditions of the loan or credit and do they suit you? For example, do you have a choice about how and where you make the repayments? If you suddenly have spare money, can you pay the loan off early without heavy penalties?

4. Can you afford the monthly payments? A more expensive loan (with a higher APR) could have lower monthly payments if they're spread out over a longer period of time. That might suit you better if your budget is tight.

Raising money checklist

Try to sort out the funding before you buy the vehicle. Some finance companies will pre-approve you or try to arrange the bank loan in principle.

Monthly payments are easily achievable in our minds, but in reality you need to stay within your limits.

Shorter loan periods are best if you can afford it as you might need another Land Rover before paying for the last one if the period is too long.

Hidden costs such as document fees and administration fees are a rip off. Try to refuse paying them and often they'll be dropped.

Credit checks are taken out on you before anyone will lend you the money. Do your own first (see page 162), as it's a waste of time deciding to buy a vehicle if you can't raise the money and it avoids the acute embarrassment of a refusal.

Dates for monthly repayments can often be chosen to suit your circumstances. Setting the date a couple of days after your pay day is often a good way of ensuring there's sufficient funding in the bank to meet the repayment when it's called for.

Paying for it

Cash

It's often said that cash (in this context actual paper money) is king when it comes to paying for a vehicle. In some situations it's the appropriate method of payment. In others it can cause great difficulties and handling it always introduces the added risk of losing it either by carelessness, fraud, or theft. Cash is really only appropriate for smaller transactions of, say, less than £500 to private individuals who don't have EPOS machines to take plastic card transactions and where it isn't really a big enough sum to warrant arranging a bank transfer. Unfortunately, it's the only 'instant' payment method available for private individuals and is the only medium for those who won't accept a cheque.

It's difficult to get hold of more than £500 without planning and giving possibly 48 hours' notice to the bank or building society that you're going to need to withdraw the cash. It's not them being difficult, it's just that in today's electronic world they don't hold much money at the branches and need notice to have the cash ready for you. You can draw it from hole in the wall machines, but again, they have limits of £250, £350, or £500 per day, depending on the type of card and machine. You can trick them by using two cards, say a debit card and a credit card to get more in one day, or you can visit the machine just before and just after midnight. Be aware that you sometimes have to pay a charge for withdrawing cash on a card, so read the small print on your credit card agreement.

It would be advisable to have a 'minder' with you whilst handling cash, especially if using a cash machine, and wear a body belt to hold the money securely. Cash is also not traceable, and if you have a problem with the vehicle in the future the recipient of the payment may prove impossible to trace. If you're selling a vehicle your bank will charge you to pay the cash in, and there's an added risk that some of it may be counterfeit.

If you pay large sums of cash into your bank or building society account you might be investigated under the 2003 Money Laundering Regulations. Auction houses and other businesses are likewise unable or unwilling to accept much more than £7,500 in cash from an individual because of these regulations, so it's unwise to accept more than this as a cash payment and impossible to use more than this as a form of payment for a vehicle in a business environment. The actual amount is up to the rules implemented by the

LEFT Cash is hard to get hold of in large quantities, especially at short notice

management of the business, but under the regulations the top limit is €15,000, which is just over £10,000 at current conversion rates, above which the company has to be registered and carry out research to establish the source of the money you're using. Company policy, for the auction or dealer, will set the limit lower than this, so that they avoid getting involved in a lot of paperwork, and usually it will be between £7,500 and £9,000. So if you unwisely intend to pay in cash you need to find out what figure the company you're dealing with has set as a maximum limit and either buy below the limit or part pay by some other means. This doesn't mean, of course, that you can't buy a vehicle for more than this, but you'll have to use a method of payment that's more traceable, such as a cheque, credit card transaction, or bank transfer.

Although in the context under discussion here cash means paper money, some people refer to a 'cash sale' as the alternative to credit when they don't actually mean they want to receive or are going to use 'folding money' as the means of payment, so if you've bought something for a cash sale check what they mean by the term 'cash' before agreeing the details.

Finance

If you're buying a vehicle from a dealer and it's going to be on finance then they'll actually pay the

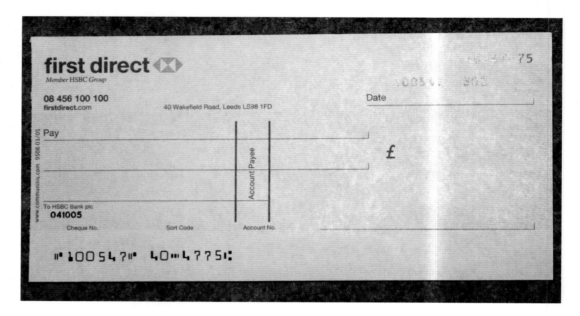

funds to the dealer. You may be asked to pay a deposit using the method most suited to both parties, usually a cheque that may need to be made out to the finance company. Alternatively the value of your trade-in may cover this.

Bank transfer

This is a simple way of paying or receiving money for a vehicle. Using the account details of the other party (their account name, bank sorting code, and account number) it's possible to transfer the money directly. It's safe, as it can't go missing, and when the vendor receives the funds they can't 'bounce' like a cheque. The transfer can be done over the internet or telephone if you have suitable accounts or by visiting your branch. There's often a fee for the transaction and it usually takes three working days to show up in the recipient's account, even though it has left yours when you set it up. Sometimes it will transfer instantly, but you need to check first to see what the situation is for the two banks involved.

Personal cheque

Personal cheques are a good medium if you're prepared to wait while the money clears in the bank. This usually takes three to five days but even if the funds look to be cleared they can be taken back up to a fortnight later if they weren't in the account it was drawn on. Besides this risk of 'bouncing' they can also be stopped by the issuing bank on the instruction of the account holder several days after they were paid in.

Building society cheque

A building society cheque is a better form of personal cheque as it's drawn against an account that's guaranteed to contain funds. The cheque therefore can't 'bounce', as the building society will only issue it if the account holds sufficient money to cover it, which is then moved into a secure holding account. It is therefore reasonably safe, though it can still be stopped by the building society on the instruction of the account holder. It can also, of course, be forged. If you withdraw a cheque from your building society and don't subsequently use it, it can be returned to your account.

Whilst high on the list of good payment methods a building society cheque isn't totally guaranteed and some vendors won't release your Land Rover until it has cleared in their account. Obtaining one requires a personal visit to your building society in working hours, so it isn't instantly accessible either. Therefore you'll probably need to pay the vendor a cash deposit to hold the vehicle. Get the vendor's details so they can be printed on the cheque, then draw the cheque from a branch of the building society and hand it over to the vendor, who may or may not let you take the vehicle there and then.

Bank draft

A bank draft is a bit of paper like a normal cheque, but it's a guaranteed item drawn on a cashiers' account at the bank into which your funds have been placed from your account. It costs a small fee to obtain one and sometimes the bank needs notice, but it can't be stopped and it won't bounce. It still takes a few working

Within the cheque image:

Leek United
BUILDING SOCIETY   50 St Edward Street Leek Staffs ST13 5DL

HSBC Bank plc   17 Derby Street Leek Staffs ST13 6HR

40-28-01

Pay

Date 31 March 06

£   750.00

Ten Thousands	Thousands	Hundreds	Tens	Units
Zero	Zero	Seven	Five	Zero

Amount of pounds in words · pence as in figures

For LEEK UNITED BUILDING SOCIETY
No. 4 ACCOUNT

A/C Payee only

68.52.15702.09/01

SIGNATORY (1)   SIGNATORY (2)

Issuing Branch

⑈884299⑈ 40⑈2801⑈

LEFT Though similar in appearance, this is a building society cheque and is guaranteed not to bounce, but it can be stopped or forged

days to clear into the recipient's account and might, of course, be stolen or forged. You also need to know the exact sum the deal will involve, though you can take a lower draft and a bit of negotiating power in cash. You need to know the recipient's name and details so these can be printed on the draft, and if you don't go ahead with the deal it can be returned into your account. Again, you need to visit the bank personally to obtain it. Bank drafts were once common in transactions but in this electronic plastic age they've almost fallen out of use.

Credit card

A credit card is a common way of paying for vehicles, even of high value. It's only usable if the vendor is in business and has an electronic point-of-sale system. The vendor doesn't necessarily need to be in the motor trade, as many other businesses can take cards. The funds are guaranteed once the transaction has been authorised, and the transfer is instant, but there's a commission charge to the recipient of, usually, between 2.5 and 4 per cent of the transaction figure, which they'll usually add to the sale price. When you're buying goods in a shop this is factored into the price on the item, but in a car sales environment it isn't so you'll usually be asked to add it to the agreed sale price. If the vehicle's not expensive it's not a lot of money if it enables you to take immediate delivery and use the credit limit on the card as a source of funds, but it's quite an expensive way of buying a vehicle. From the vendor's point of view it may be a stolen card or a fraudulent transaction, but this is becoming less likely as a result of checks on

identity and the use of chip and pin cards. If vendors follow all the proper protocols then they're fully covered in a cases of misuse.

Debit card

A debit card should be the method of choice for paying for a vehicle in all business environments. It's an instant transfer that's guaranteed from the vendor's point of view and incurs much lower charges, small enough that they'll probably cover these themselves as they have a smooth instant transaction with quick access to the funds. If the purchase takes place at an auction, where carrying large sums of cash can be risky, using a debit card allows you to take the vehicle home with you (tax, insurance, etc permitting). If buying from a dealer, it allows collection as soon as the vehicle and paperwork have been prepared for you to collect. As with credit cards, they can be stolen or used fraudulently, but if all the proper systems are followed correctly the vendor will be covered.

PayPal

Even though the sale might not have been as a result of an eBay online auction many people in this country have PayPal accounts that can be used for payments. They incur fees of about 4 per cent but it's a guaranteed payment and it gives purchasers the opportunity of using a credit card as a source of funding for something bought from a private individual. It's an ideal way of paying for an item bought through eBay and might be worth remembering as a payment option in other deals between private individuals. The purchaser, though, will probably have to pay the fees on top of the agreed price, but at least there's an audit trail for the money and it's a quick transaction. The fees aren't enormous, being only £20 on a £500 deal, so they're easily absorbed by one party or shared by both. The money request is originated through the PayPal system by the vendor and then paid by the purchaser, or can be sent by the purchaser if he knows the vendor's details. It's also quite useful with purchases from abroad as it's quick and is an easy way of coping with the conversion of UK Sterling funds into Euros or any other currency. It can also be used at the house of a vendor, using their computer as a guest without leaving any of your personal details or passwords behind. It's therefore a good method of secure instant payment.

Getting paid

If you're selling your vehicle privately it's most important that you don't end up with no vehicle and no money! In a sales situation there has to be a bit of trust on both sides, but unfortunately too much trust can often be misplaced. And even selling to what you thought was a genuine dealer can result in a duff cheque or some other problem. The only acceptable situation in which to have no car and no money is if you've sold the vehicle in a proper auction and there's a delay of a week or so whilst they check title to the vehicle and send you the cheque.

If you sell to a dealer in a straight sale make sure it's one that has proper trading premises, has been established for a long time, and is preferably local. They may be willing to transfer the money directly into your bank but will probably want to pay by cheque and won't let you keep the vehicle while it clears – even though, if the situation was reversed, they wouldn't let you drive away without the funds having cleared! You'll probably be OK, but there'll be a time lag between parting company with the vehicle and having the cleared funds available. A dealer is most unlikely to want to pay you in cash,

especially if the figure is more than a few hundred pounds. You might be able to get them to pay by bank draft, but as it puts them to quite a lot of trouble to arrange one they'll probably not want the vehicle unless you accept a cheque and give them both the vehicle and all the paperwork.

Some dealers won't want to pay you at all and will offer to sell the vehicle on your behalf. You really need to know them well and trust them as this is a risky type of trade, but you'll probably get a higher price for it than in a straight sale and you haven't got the bother of advertising it and dealing with all the people who come to view it. They may also be reluctant to pay you out fully even when your vehicle has gone, especially if they've had to take another vehicle in a trade. It's useful to draw up a simple agreement covering sales price and who's responsible for the costs of advertising and any warranty work, etc, so that both parties know where they stand. Check the insurance position as well if you've transferred yours to your replacement vehicle.

If you're selling privately then insist on cash or cleared funds before you release the vehicle. If the purchaser wants to pay by building society cheque or bank draft the issuing branch's telephone number is usually on these, and so long as the branch vouches for the authenticity of the cheque or draft then it's usually safe to release the vehicle. An inter-bank transfer is really the safest way of getting the money, though some purchasers can't or won't want to wait the three working days for you to receive it.

Always remember that though it would be nice to think that you can trust people, when it comes to money matters you rarely can.

VAT

Value Added Tax is applied to most things that we buy. It's charged at the full rate of (currently) 17.5 per cent on new cars but it's included in the price and not shown as a separate item unless you look

BELOW Commercials such as this attract VAT in commercial sales. Make certain you know the full cost before bidding or agreeing a purchase on a vehicle

more deeply into how the showroom windscreen price is calculated. Some Land Rover products are regarded as commercial vehicles and if purchased by a VAT-registered user the tax can be reclaimed. These are therefore displayed as '£X + VAT'.

Land Rovers that fall into this category are the commercial van and Pick Up types of all models and the 12-seat Defender Station Wagon, which is classified as a bus and therefore a commercial vehicle. So if, for example, you buy a Defender van from a farmer the invoice will show a price plus VAT. If you bought the same vehicle from a private individual who was not VAT registered then there would be no separate VAT to pay, though the vehicle might be more expensive as the seller would not have been able to reclaim the tax.

Dealers selling Land Rovers classed as 'cars' don't charge VAT on them, though they have to pay a portion of their mark-up as VAT. If they sell Land Rovers classed as 'commercials' they may be displayed as 'plus VAT' if bought from a registered user, or sometimes – if they've been bought in from an unregistered private individual – they're sold on again under a special scheme and there's no separate VAT to pay, as they'll deal with this in their mark-up as with a 'car'.

It pays to read the advertisement well or listen very carefully to the auctioneer if you're trying to purchase a commercial Land Rover variant at auction. The Land Rover you just thought cheap at £10,000 on the fall of the hammer won't be so cheap at £11,750 once the tax has been added to the invoice, so read the catalogue and listen when the details are read out before the lot is sold. They usually have a 'Plus VAT' sticker on the windscreen as well.

Selling a vehicle that's on finance

Most people who buy new or recent vehicles either can't afford all the money or choose not to pay for the vehicle in one go and have the vehicle on some sort of finance. Broadly speaking there are two sorts of finance arrangement: hire purchase and lease, though there can be modifications of the latter to resemble the former. In both cases, though, the person with the vehicle isn't the legal owner – even though their name is on the paperwork and registration document – and they can't really sell it as they don't have good title to it.

In a HP deal the purchaser pays a deposit and

the finance company puts up the rest of the money. The purchaser then has use of the vehicle while making monthly payments to the finance company to pay off the balance. In law the vehicle belongs to the finance company until the last payment has been made, when title transfers to the user.

A leased vehicle always belongs in law to the finance company, to whom it's handed back after, usually, 36 months. The deposit paid and the monthly payments are just a hire charge, even though the user's name is usually on the paperwork and the registration document, as he's the registered keeper. Sometimes the user has the option of buying the vehicle after the end of its rental period by means of a 'balloon payment'. He then becomes the legal owner.

As you don't own an HP or lease vehicle you can't sell them, though many people try. The only correct way to do this is to pay off the outstanding balances and the vehicle is then yours to sell. If you trade a vehicle in with finance owing on it the dealer will do this and in effect add the outstanding amount to the money borrowed for the replacement, as long as it doesn't leave your deposit too small to obtain new finance. It's a good idea and polite to make them aware of the fact before they run a check and find out, as they may not want to do this, especially as they may have to lay out a lot of money.

If you want to get rid of a lease vehicle then you hand it back to the lease company, who will often charge a termination fee depending on how far into the agreement you are. Termination at the front end of a deal is always expensive. Some people advertise to buy the remaining portion of the lease from you and undertake to pay the rest of the payments but this isn't strictly legal and if they don't pay or the vehicle gets damaged or goes missing it falls you to make good the missing money.

If you need to sell a vehicle that's on HP get in contact with the finance company and agree the way forward before you do so. If it's because of a change in circumstances, such as the loss of a job so that you can't pay, approach them before you run into difficulties, not when a few payments have been bounced by the bank. The people at the finance company are human and will be much easier to deal with if you tell them sooner rather than later that you're having problems, as the last thing they want to do is to repossess their vehicle from you. That's the last thing you want too, as you'll probably lose any money you might otherwise have got if the vehicle was sold in a controlled manner.

Some will want you to sell to a dealer, possibly the supplying one, or at an auction house of their choice, and will take the money due for the vehicle and either reimburse you with any extra money over and above the settlement figure if there is any, or else ask you to make up the shortfall if there isn't. It's not them being mean, but a vehicle is usually worth less than the outstanding balance owing on it until the last third or so of the finance period. This is because the cost of the finance is divided equally over the period whilst the value, especially of a new vehicle, drops rapidly at first then more slowly as time progresses. This is especially true of low deposit deals with balloon payments at the end, as they're pretty much calculated so that the value and the outstanding balance – the balloon payment – are the same at the end of the deal.

Other finance companies will let you sell the vehicle on their behalf if the cheque is made out to them for the full amount or at least for the settlement figure. They'll only remove it from the finance database when the money has cleared in their account. You need to tell the purchaser that this is going on, as you need them to make out two cheques. It will also show up on the finance database as being on HP, and even though the buyer will have parted with the money and got the vehicle they don't have good title until your finance company issues a letter to the effect that it's all paid off. It's perceived as very risky from a purchaser's point of view, though in reality it isn't, and few will dare to proceed. It also involves trust between the three parties, which is difficult to gain. What you must never do is sell the vehicle and pocket the money yourself even if you continue to make the payments, as it's illegal and will probably end up with you in court.

If you decide to pay off the outstanding settlement figure in one go before selling the vehicle get a letter confirming that the vehicle is now yours, as it takes a few weeks to be removed from the database and you can show the purchaser the letter before they run a check and find it listed even though it's clear.

Loans from other sources – banks, building societies, etc – will probably not be placed against your car as they're a loan to you personally for the purpose of buying a car, though they'll probably be recorded against your house. If you have a bank loan to buy your car you probably own the vehicle and have good title. If the money was given to you and you paid for the car it's not HP. A finance company will always pay the dealer directly, as in law it's they who are buying the vehicle and not you. If, therefore, the full amount has passed through your account there's no problem selling the vehicle, as it's your property; likewise, there's no compulsion to pay the money back if you keep up the payments, as it's a personal loan. You can therefore buy another car with it. You don't need not tell prospective purchasers as it won't be on a finance database, and it's a lot better as it's a cleaner deal and unlikely to put them off buying. If you don't know whether or not you own a car or if it's on the finance database find out by reading the agreement you signed or ask the lender.

If you buy a vehicle on which the vendor tells you there's outstanding finance, or if you find it yourself when checking, it's fine to carry on and buy it. You need the vendor to tell you the contact details for the company involved and the agreement reference number and follow their instructions. The vendor will also need to tell you the amount you need to put on the cheque for the finance company, as the finance company can't tell you but will confirm a figure if you give it to them. It's best if you're together when initiating contact with the finance company, as the vendor can give his permission for the finance company to deal with you. In this situation an inter-bank transfer is the best form of payment, or else your credit or debit card, as it's an instant transaction and you aren't left in limbo land for several days. Therefore set a transfer up beforehand and suggest paying the finance company over the phone just before or as you collect the vehicle, possibly at the vendor's house so that they can confirm it's paid, and pay the residual balance to the vendor by inter-bank transfer in a building society cheque or bank draft, or else in cash if it's the only acceptable method to satisfy the vendor. Then take the vehicle away with you.

This way it's the vendor that has to trust you and not you who has to trust the vendor. They might not like the idea, but it's a small risk they'll have to take in order to unburden themselves of the vehicle. As it's going to involve more work for you I'd expect a bonus in the form of a discounted price. The vendor's only other option is to sell into the trade or auction the vehicle, so you should be heading down to the sort of figure they'd receive from an auction after all the selling charges have been taken into account. So if you're confident enough to buy like this and put up with the hassle then be brave enough to bid a really low price.

kia

KIA SPORTAGE KARMEN 2.0

1998, Limited edition, tax, full m.o.t, 70,000 miles, full electric kit, immobiliser, CD player, sunroof, tow bar, GOOD CONDITION.

£2,800 o.n.o.
Tel. 01782 914378.

undai

I COUPE 1.6

52,000, 5 months tax, full m.o.t., TION, REAL EYE CATCHER

00 o.n.o.

LAND ROVER RANGEROVER

2.5 DSE, blue, 97, R reg., 6 months m.o.t and tax, good cond., 2 recent tyres, high miles, quick sale hence

£5,500 o.n.o.
Tel. 07967 632887 (m).
01782 619811.
NO CANVASSERS

MITSUBISHI PAJERO

SWB, 2.5 auto diesel, imported Setup 2003, one owner, T reg, two-tone grey metallic, genuine 66,000 miles, taxed and m.o.t., immaculate for year, no rust, all usual extras, genuine calls only, no canvassers.
Private sale.

£2,900 o.n.o
Tel. 01630 672437.

LAND ROVER 110 COUNTY

1986, 2.5 petrol, 97,000 original miles m.o.t's going back to 97, never let me down, 10 months m.o.t., reluctant sale

£2,050 o.n.o.

(R)
All cars c
So
Part
Te

NIS

ex
one
relia
lo

£
Tel.

ES
1995

Tel.
07

V
CA
7 Se
2
tw
alar
t
ta

full service history,
very good condition,

£650 o.n.o.

Tel. 01782 857636.

ICRA

ge,
dition,
m new,
irst car,
ance,
06,
6,

n.o.

813(m)

AN
RA

Diesel,
s m.o.t.,
ax,
ion,

529 or
57(m)

AN
TE

IBUS
V reg.,
hite,
oors,
ocking,
ws,
es,
sted,

RENAULT
ESPACE

N reg.,
taxed/tested July,
2 litre Natasp diesel,
taxed July,

£1,050 o.n.o

Tel. 01889 590137.

RENAULT
ESPACE

P reg.,
tested end May,
2 litre turbo diesel.

£1,350 o.n.o.

Tel. 01889 590137.

RENAULT
MEGANE COUPE

1.4, 16 valve, Sport,
1999, T reg., 69,000 miles,
taxed, 12 months m.o.t, 17 inch
alloys, excellent condition.

£2,950 o.n.o

Tel. 01782 876681 or

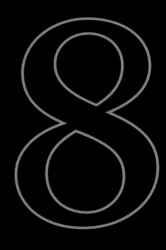

Advertisements

Reading between the lines

If this sentence was a 'For Sale' advertisement it would need to have got all the salient points across by *now*. This is because people decide if a vehicle is of interest to them after reading the first 20 words. If their interest has been drawn in that time, they'll go on to read chapter and verse to get a better mental picture, but even then they'll only want to digest the relevant points and won't be interested in flowery prose.

When composing an advert it's best to list the good selling points, and in order to establish these you need to put yourself in the purchaser's shoes. Then rewrite these points as phrases to be listed after the basic description. Only list positive points, and whilst you can't misrepresent the vehicle you can massage the truth. For instance, if the vehicle has, say, nine months' MoT left to run, or more than six months' road tax, these can be legitimately described as 'long tax and MoT', as this is a positive attribute; but if it only has a month left on each it's unwise to list it as 'short tax and MoT', as this is a negative attribute. It would be far better just to say 'tax and MoT', as this is neutral. Keep away from words and phrases such as 'Bargain', 'First to see will buy', 'Good condition for year', 'Rare', or any similar expressions of opinion that aren't fact. Even some facts need to be left out: '£3,740 spent on maintenance, bills to prove' may be true, but it gives the subliminal impression of a money pit.

Don't waste space on the number of owners unless it genuinely is 50 years old and only had one owner. Most vehicles change hands every two or three years so previous multiple ownership is to be expected. 'Four owners' makes no positive contribution to selling, as one owner may have been a car rental firm and another Ebenezer Scrooge.

Other things to miss out include 'must sell, moving house', 'divorce forces sale', 'new vehicle arriving' or any other personalisation which might suggest you're vulnerable to a low offer. Similarly, 'reluctant sale' or 'much loved' will put uncertainty in the mind of the reader, who'll wonder why it's being sold and therefore what's wrong with it. Just stick to the salient points needed to encourage a potential purchaser to make contact.

If the registration age identifier is a positive point, being the newest for the year (ie a '53' not an '03'), then put it in early. If it's not and is therefore a slightly negative point put it in later, as the purchaser might not put so much weight on it by then. Thus, if our example had been a K-reg we would have included it; but as it's 'J' we've omitted it from the first 20 words.

Don't put in negative statements that have a qualifying 'because' in them. 'Cheap because of short MoT' or 'Low price because high mileage' should be avoided. Just put the true mileage and the price – let purchasers draw their own conclusions, otherwise you're likely to get a reduced offer because of a negative aspect you've already allowed for in your price.

Don't list every feature the vehicle has, especially standard-fit items. Power steering, for example, is standard on a Discovery so need not be listed, but it was optional on old 90s dating to the early 1980s so ought to be listed. And don't list all the items the model type features, just the main ones. An ES Discovery has lots of trim differences and body enhancements but the only ones worth listing are climate control and heated leather seats.

Never use shorthand for the items you wish to emphasise, as even if the reader knows what they are you'll be diverting their attention whilst they figure them out. It looks a bit dealer-like as well and might make them think you're operating as a disguised dealer. So don't use acronyms such as ICE, ETC, HDC, AC, FSH, GWO, and T&T. It is, however, acceptable to use model identification acronyms that are commonly used and understood, such as TDI and EFI, since spelling

them out in full can divert brainpower into translating them back into recognisable acronyms! MoT and LPG are likewise acceptable, as are abbreviations such as 'Auto', 'Air Con', and 'CD', which are all in common everyday use.

Be careful of the use of 're-' words – rebuilt, reconditioned, refurbished, resprayed, repaired, replaced – as they all have different meanings and even more interpretations in people's minds, and they all tend to raise more questions than they answer. 'Replacement engine fitted', for instance: was it new from Land Rover, or a 150,000-mile example from a scrap yard? 'Chassis repaired': was it with a new half-chassis professionally welded on, or with baked bean tins glued on with bodyfiller? So only use 're-' words if they're an easily interpreted positive attribute.

'New engine fitted by main dealer 15,000 miles ago under warranty (paperwork to confirm)' is probably just about worth putting in, but even that can set off negative thoughts about unreliability so may be best left to the secondary questioning stage, which usually comes with the telephone call before viewing.

An example of how the first part of an advert needs to start is therefore:

1992 LAND ROVER DEFENDER 110 COUNTY STATION WAGON.

12 seats, 200TDI diesel engine, galvanised chassis, good tyres, long MoT £4,000.

This gives the model type, age, the price, and other positive points, all within 20 words. If you're advertising in some publications you can even leave out 'Land Rover', as amongst the cognoscenti in a Land Rover magazine you don't need to waste valuable words telling them what it is and can use the space to get more relevant information into view, such as 'good bulkhead'. But if it's in a local weekly paper you need to identify your vehicle, and if it's an internet auction you need to put it in the title so that it'll be picked up in a search.

Whilst it costs money to advertise, the value of these first words isn't financial. They're bait, and you need the right bait to get potential purchasers on the hook before you can reel them in. Never *ever* put in 'O.N.O.' ('or near offer'), as it immediately signals you're ready to drop the price and will be bid on a lot lower than if you just put a price. Also don't put in 'no offers', as this will also put potential purchasers off. Just stick to giving the asking price. I personally don't like the '£999' trick either, as I spend brainpower saying to myself 'That means a thousand pounds', and it diverts my attention from the rest of the advert. It also looks semi-professional, so just stick to whole numbers or significant fractions of the units we're dealing in, such as £6,750.

Sometimes colour is a positive point, and popular colours such as 'Metallic black' and 'Bonatti grey' are worth including in the first 20 words. If the vehicle is a negative colour from a selling point of view, such as white, then leave it out. Similarly, leather seats are a plus selling point, cloth seats a neutral point, and vinyl seats a negative point, even in commercial vehicles, so only include the trim type if it's leather.

An automatic gearbox is a plus point so put that in. If you don't put in 'Auto' then it's assumed it's manual, which you can confirm later on. Jot down other plus points such as air conditioning or climate control, winch, etc. Don't list them all at the start of the advert, as there isn't enough room, but writing them down will let you sort out which to include and which to list later. Play around with the order as well. Perhaps 'Galvanised chassis, 200TDI diesel engine, 12 seats' would be a better order, as these points change importance as a vehicle ages.

Once you're happy with the first part of your advert you can move on to the secondary attributes and if necessary expand on some of the ones already touched upon:

'J registration 5 door full County Specification, white in colour with 12 grey cloth seats. Seatbelts on front six seats. 5 speed gearbox. Chassis replaced two years ago with new galvanised. 92,000 miles with full service history. Cam belt replaced at 72K miles, all bills available to confirm. Bulkhead sound. Michelin XZY tyres less than half worn with unused spare. MoT tested until middle of September. Taxed until end of June. Inspection welcome.'

Again, just stick to the facts and include the negative points as well.

Next you need the contact details. Don't be shy, as if you can't be contacted people will quickly move on. Give several methods such as daytime phone, evening phone, mobile, and even an email address. But only numbers you can actually be contacted on. Make certain your employer doesn't mind you taking personal calls at work and only give a work number with their permission. If you have a switchboard tell them too, so they know who to put the call through to when someone rings about a Land Rover for sale. Try to always give a land line number, as it makes people feel more confident about purchasing

something. If you're hard to contact leave an answering machine on and ring people back.

Lastly, include details of where the vehicle is located. You don't need to be too specific, but if advertising nationally give an area, such as 'North Derbyshire', or a town or city, such as 'Luton', or directions such as '2 miles Junction 6 M1', so that a potential purchaser can make an informed decision as to whether they want to travel or not.

If possible in the advertising medium you're using include a photograph of the vehicle. A three-quarter front view is always best and helps the potential purchaser to visualise the vehicle.

Our finished advert ought to look like this:

1992 LAND ROVER DEFENDER 110 COUNTY STATION WAGON

12 seats, 200TDI diesel engine, galvanised chassis, good tyres, long MoT

£4,000

J registration 5 door full County Specification, white in colour with 12 grey cloth seats. Seatbelts on front six seats. 5 speed gearbox. Chassis replaced two years ago with new galvanised. 92,000 miles with full service history. Cam belt replaced at 72K miles, all bills available to confirm. Bulkhead sound. Michelin XZY tyres less than half worn with unused spare. MoT tested until middle of September. Taxed until end of June. Inspection welcome.

01234 567890 weekdays 09876 543210 weekends and evening after 7 pm (North Derbyshire).

Buying from an advertisement

An advertisement for a Land Rover, whether in a daily, weekly or monthly publication, in a shop window, or on the internet, will reveal a lot more about the vendor than they possibly realise. As the potential purchaser it's up to you to glean as much information as possible to help you decide if the vehicle is suitable for your requirements. This is the first step in a long and sometimes torturous process that may or may not end up with you purchasing a Land Rover. It's also one of the points at which you have to make a 'go, no go' decision.

It's a good idea to read as many advertisements as you can, including ones for Land Rovers that aren't even on your list of potential purchases, as it's part of an educational process getting you practised in how to read adverts and how to pick out vehicles you might purchase. It's also a way of spotting traders pretending to be private vendors, as they may well have more than one vehicle for sale in the same publication and you'll probably spot the familiar phone number.

One of the first things you need to ascertain is the trading status of the advertiser. Under the 'Business Advertisements (Disclosures) Order 1977' it's a legal requirement of the person placing the advert to disclose if they're a trader selling goods – in this case vehicles – in the course of business and to make the fact clear to the reader. They also need to indicate if VAT is included in the asking price or will be levied on top if appropriate.

The trade disclosure requirement is there because consumer protection law is different for private or trade sales and purchasers need to know if they're purchasing with or without the protection of these laws. The disclosure may be obvious if the advert has 'Blogg's Garage' as a banner. The word 'Trade' may also appear at the end, or sometimes just a 'T'. But many professional motor traders pretend to be private vendors in order to avoid any of the liabilities they may have as professionals, and possibly to avoid having to pay income tax or to be VAT registered. Mobile phones make it quite easy to hide your identity and many adverts therefore have just a mobile number. It's much more reassuring to see a land line number listed as well.

Such quasi traders often give themselves away in adverts as they can't help using phrases such

Land Rover Lightweight V6 fitted Ford V6, Weber carb, needs slight attention for MOT £800 ono. Tel ███████ (Staffordshire)

Range Rover 3.5 V8 manual, solid chassis, body ok, new mud-terrian tyres & starter, 2" lift and diff guard, needs MOT ₣900. Tel ███████

2000 Defender 90 Heritage Limited Edition green leather seats, SS exhaust, air con, sunroof, fold up rear step, rear bumperettes, fold back spare wheel carrier, BFG/AT's, adjustable height tow pack, remote alarm, CD/radio, alloys, re-Waxoyled recently, mechanically sound, runs extremely well, economical, (averages 30 mpg) high mileage 118k hence low price £13,000 very reluctant sale, but it's too good to off-road. ████

ABOVE These are all reasonably well constructed and average about 20 words. They give the points needed and include the location. Two of them have 'ONO' after the price and this is to be avoided at all costs. As a purchaser it gives an opportunity to trim the price before and after viewing by asking 'would you take X for it?' So remember 'NO, NO, ONO' when placing an advert, and as a buyer start the price reduction as soon as you can!

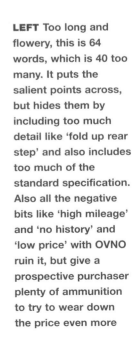

LEFT Too long and flowery, this is 64 words, which is 40 too many. It puts the salient points across, but hides them by including too much detail like 'fold up rear step' and also includes too much of the standard specification. Also all the negative bits like 'high mileage' and 'no history' and 'low price' with OVNO ruin it, but give a prospective purchaser plenty of ammunition to try to wear down the price even more

RIGHT Slightly too long, and the picture shows it is a double cab with tread plates so do we need it in the words as well? It is a bit difficult to decide if £11,900 + vat is more attractive than £14,000 inc vat, but at least it is clear that it would be reclaimable by a registered purchaser. From the wording, this sounds like a dealer describing a vehicle so establish the basis for the sale before even looking at it

Land Rover Defender 110 County TD5 Double Cab
colour Bonati Grey, 2495cc, registered 2002, mileage 83,000 FSH, Warn winch, heavy duty springs, tomb raider features, full chequer plate kit, BF Goodrich tyres £14,000 [inc vat] Tel

RIGHT Too long and has the 're' word in that is open to different interpretations. It includes details like the period of restoration, which is irrelevant in an advert, and hints at a forced sale situation, inviting low offers. The vendor must know his bottom line selling price so ought to include it. I got bored by the fifth line and moved on to the next ad, as will many other potential buyers. As a buyer, however, it will not get a big response so it is perhaps worth a call to discuss the vehicle and see if a deal could be worked out.

A beautiful Lady, Lovingly restored, Historic 1958 Series 2, classic cream and green finish, No tax bracket, low insurance, unleaded, brought back to its original glory by Landrover Specialist over a period of 3 years, all authentic parts used, must be seen. Sale only due to imminent posting abroad. Have been offered a good deal of money just for the registration. Offers please to Brian on

as 'clean vehicle' or using tradespeak shorthand – '44K miles with history', 'Traction', 'EW', 'FSH' – and they tend to list all the standard features of a model that most owners don't even know are fitted or have forgotten are there – 'ABS, Heated Seats, Air con'. They also usually give the name of the colour, which again most people don't know beyond it being green, red, or whatever. But dealers often say 'IN White' or 'Davos White', where a private individual would just say 'white'. There's nothing wrong with buying from a trader, but if they're not disclosing they are one what else are they hiding? It's much better to buy from a properly operated business that discloses and displays its details everywhere as it's legally obliged to, and is sufficiently confident you'll be happy with your purchase that it puts its name on the back window and the spare wheel cover.

The VAT disclosure requirement is there so that you know the exact price of vehicles regarded for VAT purposes as commercials. £10,000 might mean just that or it might be £11,750 if it's plus tax (17.5 per cent at time of writing) or £8,510 plus tax if it's already included.

As you read on through the advert there could be several aspects that might make you move on to the next one. Is it the desired type of Land Rover? Does it meet the other criteria you've set – such as colour, age, mileage, price, and fuel type – or is a compromise achievable? Is it located within a convenient distance for inspection and collection? Many adverts don't give a location but a reverse code list will identify the area the phone is located in. Whilst you can usually get what you want within a convenient range some more obscure vehicles, such as the limited editions, will involve a journey to wherever you can find one. Look at the photograph that's hopefully been included. Though you may not see a lot it does help the visualisation process. Pictures on the internet will usually show more detail than those in printed media but be aware that vehicles usually look better in a picture than in the metal, so take this into account before bidding.

Make a list of advertised vehicles that you're interested in following up and then re-read all the details. This will probably allow you to narrow the list even further and pick out target vehicles. It's best to deal with one vehicle at a time and to pursue that line of inquiry until it's successful or you reach a 'no go' decision. In the meantime you can be researching a couple more to fall back on if your first choice falls through. I'd strongly advise you not to have too many enquiries going on at the same time as you'll confuse the facts and information. Three is plenty to be juggling at one time and if you've done your research properly you'll probably buy one of them. In fact if you've done your homework properly you'll only need to look at one vehicle. Don't pay any attention to those who say 'never buy the first one you see', as if it fits all your criteria and comes from a reputable source you'd be foolish not to buy it.

People who traipse around loads of dealers saying they can't find the vehicle they want are doing something wrong. All too often phrases such as 'none of them would offer me enough money for mine' or 'they're all too expensive' are heard, suggesting to me that the potential purchaser hasn't done any research and is out of touch with reality. You really do need to stay in the game and keep up to date with values when either buying or selling. Read the relevant publications and check on the internet regularly, as a vehicle that's cheaper, more suitable, nearer, or whatever, might turn up at any time and can be added to your list of main contenders whilst the others are put on hold, discarded, or placed in reserve.

Once you've found a few possible vehicles to target you need to get on the telephone. Don't delay in doing this because as soon as a new publication reaches the newsagents' shelves other people are out there looking for the same vehicle as you, and if you're looking at a time when the market is buoyant all the worthwhile vehicles tend to get sold quite quickly. So you have to regard it as a race with only one winner, and that needs to be you.

Land Rover 109 Stage 1 V8
3.5l pickup, 1980, VGC, re-chassied 2002, MOT August 2006, reluctant sale £1,850 ono. Tel ▃▃▃▃▃ (Derby)

Land Rover Discovery 11-93 L
80,500 miles, white, 3 doors, new wheels, tyres, brake discs, no welds, undersealed £3,740 spent on maintenance over the last 9 years, all MOT certs & receipts, 12 months MOT, 9 months Tax, good conditiion £2,800. Tel ▃▃▃▃▃

(Scotland)

TOP LEFT This is short enough, but a photograph would make it more interesting and it would be better to leave out 'reluctant sale' and 'ono'. From a purchaser's perspective, it is a rare model and worthy of investigation as it is cheap if properly described. It is worth asking if the vendor can email you some pictures in a situation like this, especially if you live far away.

LEFT Too long at over 40 words. We do not need to read all about new this and that, and £3,700 spent on maintenance in last 9 years. However, knowing if it is a V8 petrol or TDI diesel would be much better information.

Defender 90 TD5 CSW 1999
(T), 36,000miles, FLSH, cobar blue, BFG M/T's, PAS, T/C, ABS, A/con, sunroof, A bar, spots, tow pack, alarm/immobilisor, steering guard, 10 stack CD, T+T, lady owner, excellent con'd £12,000. Tel 01702 23▃▃ Nic (Essex)

Discovery 300Tdi Safari Auto
1999, T reg, 56,000miles with history, T+T, E/W, A/C, cruise, pas, C/L, heated F/screen, 7 seats, ladder, tow pack, twin roof's , 5 new BFG A/T's, with extras, VGC £8250. Tel 01702 23▃▃ nic (Essex)

Defender 90 Hard Top 1985 2.25 petrol, 55K miles, very smart and very well maintained, Taxed May 06, full MOT, new front seats, 5 good tyres, very clean inside and out, excellent mechanics, very quiet and straight driving, used daily, company 90 forces sale £1,995 no offers. Tel Chris ▃▃▃▃▃ (Coventry)

This sounds a bit 'dealerspeak' with T&T, Tow pack, ABS and so on, but there is no trade declaration

Further on we come across this one with the same telephone number, suggesting a trader, so we need to be very wary

The 'company 90 forces sale' bit should not be included as it signals a soft target in a forced sale

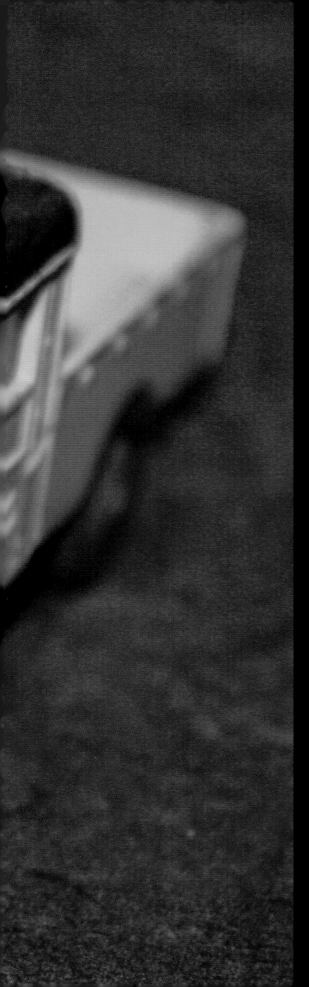

Negotiating as a buyer and seller

Perhaps the hardest part of buying or selling a vehicle is negotiating the price. It really comes to the fore in straight deals, as in a trade-in deal you'll probably have to accept what you're offered if you want to go ahead, as there'll be very little room for movement.

In this country we aren't used to dealing. It's something we're only confronted with when it comes to buying and selling houses and motor vehicles, so most people aren't good at it. We don't haggle for things and tend to just pay the asking price, or shop elsewhere if we aren't happy with what we're expected to pay. Yet we have this notion that we shouldn't pay the asking price for the two most expensive purchases in our lives, cars and houses, and feel we must indulge in a bit of horse-trading to reach a figure acceptable to both parties before the deal can move on. As a nation, however, we lack the interpersonal skills and the ability to read body language that would enable us to do this properly, and usually end up feeling that we could have paid less or got more. The main problem is that we don't get much practice, since most people only buy three or four

houses and perhaps 16 cars in their lives and tend to forget any lessons that were learnt years earlier when it comes to the next purchase or sale.

One of the hardest things to judge from a vendor's point of view is whether you have a 'messer' or a 'live buyer' on your hands. If you're bad at reading body language treat everyone as a live buyer until proven wrong. Look for physical signs as well, such as turning up with a trailer or having a bag that might contain cash. And don't be frightened of asking questions about payment methods and collections before doing a deal. The old adage of a bird in the hand etc can be translated to a man in your yard with cash and a trailer being worth two on the telephone.

As a buyer, never assume the vendor is a full time salesman, though you should treat them as though they're the most experienced motor dealer

in the world until you get the feedback to suggest they're not and that it may be possible to gain the upper hand in the negotiations. Even a sales person working for a dealer may not be the seasoned professional you imagine.

The first thing to remember as a seller is to only negotiate on the price after the potential purchaser has satisfied himself that he wants to proceed. This is because you only want one round of bidding. If the vehicle has been properly valued in the first place you should not have to drop your asking price just to attract viewings. If you drop the asking price at such an early stage the potential buyer may then try to get a further reduction after inspecting the vehicle, justifying this with a 'because', as in 'because it needs new tyres, 'it's high mileage', or whatever. So it's much better from a vendor's viewpoint to have only one round of negotiations, with the potential purchaser taking all the 'becauses' on board right from the start.

As a purchaser, however, it's much better to have two bites at the cherry if possible, and to start chipping at the price before leaving home. Asking a seller if he'd take £9,000 for a £10,000 vehicle will get either a 'yes' or 'no' reply, neither of which stops you from viewing it and having another go at chipping away from the lower starting point.

Secondly, remember that you can't be both buyer and seller at the same time, so if you're selling get the other party to make an offer, which you'll initially probably decline. Don't drop the asking price yourself – you might say of a £1,000 advertised price 'I'll take £750 for it', when the buyer might have been prepared to give as much as £900 but will now try for an even better bargain by saying 'I was thinking more of £600.'

As a purchaser, though, you should try to get the vendor to make the first drop so that you can whittle it down further. The question 'What's your best price?' or 'What will you take for it' should come before an actual offer, as you might offer more than they'd have asked for. If they won't play along make an insultingly low offer, as that'll usually get them to put a starting price on the table. Then when you do make a more realistic offer go in lower than your top price so that there's room for them to push you up a little.

Be very careful with the words you use if you're forced to suggest a price first, so as not to actually make it an offer. 'Would you take £X' is a question and in no way means you'll be buying the vehicle, even though it might imply so, and it isn't seen as an insult so much as a more formal way of saying 'I'll give you such-and-such for it'. Starting the 'Would you take…' game on the phone is a good way of seeing if the vendor will come down to the proper price before you leave home to look, as if not it's a waste of your time and fuel.

Sometimes a really low price suggestion gets a surprising result and still doesn't commit you to buying. The question 'Would you take £9,500' as the opening gambit on the phone over a £12,500 asking price might get you a surprising 'Yes' answer, in which case you can possibly even agree to buy it sight unseen, qualified by 'If it's as you've described it'. I've even arranged bank transfer payment to previously unknown people for unseen vehicles under such circumstances, as you need to act quickly before they have a chance to change their mind or get higher offers from other interested parties. You can't back out,

though, or try to renegotiate the price when you see the vehicle unless they've been 'economical with the truth' in the description and it's genuinely not as described. However, I'd advise you to only take this sort of risk with a private vendor, as it's easier to get your money back if their description is inaccurate. If a dealer, especially one with marginal business ethics, has your money you'll find it difficult to get it back no matter how they described the vehicle, and since in law it's likely to be regarded as a trade sale and sold as seen you'll probably have no comeback there either.

Even though I've had success buying this way I wouldn't recommend you to try it, and though I wouldn't normally recommend handling large sums of 'folding money' either it's possibly appropriate in such a case as it's easier to take it home again if the vehicle isn't as you were led to believe.

Thirdly, pay no heed to the 'I've been offered more than that already' or 'It's cost me more than that' sort of line as a way of getting you to up the bid. If it's genuinely not worth more reply with 'Well you should have taken it' or 'That's your problem not mine' as you leave. Similarly, if you're selling ignore 'I can buy one for less than that from such-and-such' or 'There's another one in the paper for £X' statements, as they're unlikely to be true. These are all ways of softening you up for the price hit.

Fourthly, as a buyer don't indulge in rounds of attempted price reductions just for the sake of it. Though we're all keen for a bargain there's nothing wrong in *not* attempting to batter a price. If the vehicle is genuinely worth what's being asked don't be afraid to pay it. The vendor is probably well aware of the condition and if he's priced the vehicle properly he'll have taken everything into account, so don't try to justify further reductions for the same things. A vehicle may be priced at £10,000 when it would normally be £12,000 because it's high mileage, so don't try to justify a bid of £8,000 by saying it's high mileage as you'll be wasting everyone's time.

Often you get the feeling that a price is non-negotiable, or you might have been told on the phone or in the advert 'No offers'. Under such circumstances either pay the money or, if it's genuinely not worth the asking price, say you'd have bought it but only see it as being worth £X so you're unable to make a deal. This gives the vendor the opportunity to drop the price if he wants to. Never try to force the issue, as people with fixed prices are usually dogmatic about them and a challenge is rarely successful. I never really believe people can't be moved on the price and if something I want is genuinely overpriced I'll try to demonstrate its true value to them with valid points and let them make the move. Often the people you're dealing with in such cases aren't used to selling or buying and have seen a similar Land Rover for sale at the same price elsewhere without realising that theirs isn't of the same status. This is especially true of project vehicles, especially if they've invested money and time in them. Likewise, if you've overvalued something be prepared to come down to its proper value.

Lastly, treat the other party with respect and be polite. Treat them as you'd wish to be treated yourself if the situation was reversed. Don't be cold; talk to them about the weather, life, the universe, or anything else, but not about yourself or why you're buying or selling the Land Rover. The other party doesn't need chapter and verse of your life story as it just gets in the way of the matter in hand, and you might give away something significant that exposes a chink in your armour. Letting out the fact that you're desperate for the money, that your wife has given you an ultimatum to sell it, or that the bank manager is sending you rude letters is the biggest gift a wily bidder can have. Likewise, if you're the buyer don't tell the vendor that you're booked to go on holiday next week and there'll be six of you in the Mini if you don't buy something, or that you need to tow the daughter's pony to a gymkhana on Saturday. Such things will lead them to suspect that they may be in a very strong bargaining position – and they are!

Always keep your cards firmly face down on the table throughout the game. When it's over and they're counting the money or writing out the receipt it's fine to let on why you wanted that particular vehicle. As a seller, 'surplus to requirements' truthfully covers all the reasons there are for selling a vehicle if the question is asked.

To successfully conduct a deal, then, you need to fix both an optimum price and the maximum price you'll buy for or the minimum you'll sell for, and stick rigidly to them. You must try to get the other party to do the running with the figures.

There's an accepted way of resolving things if the negotiations grind to a halt and that's to meet the other party half way, agreeing a price that's half-way between the last offer and the last asking price. Some dealers have been known to flick a coin when deciding amongst themselves if the deal is to be done at the asking price or the offer price! Thus if £1,000 is the asking price and £600 is the offer on the table, in order to conclude the deal one party – usually the vendor, if they're prepared to accept the figure – will say that they'll meet you half-way and accept £800. So as a

purchaser it's best to bid up in small increments to the figure which is below your limit by the same amount as the vendor's is above it. Thus if he's stuck at £2,000 and you'll give £1,750, don't rise above a bid of £1,500.

Bid increases and price reductions need to be in units that reflect the size of the figures involved. Think in units of approximately 5 per cent initially and 2.5 per cent for larger figures as you get nearer to a deal. So bidding on a £10,000 Land Rover might start at £8,000 and increase in units of £500 and then £250 to settle at possibly £9,250. With cheaper Land Rovers think in units of approximately 10 per cent and 5 per cent, so that a vehicle advertised for £1,250 would probably move from an initial offer in units of £100 and then £50. It's just a waste of everyone's time to increase a bid by, say, £100 in negotiations for a £30,000 Range Rover, as it's only 0.33 per cent of the price; but the same figure of £100 is far too big an amount by which a bid for a £500 Land Rover should be increased, since it's as much as 20 per cent of the price.

Sometimes it's better to negotiate in kind as well. If you can't get the price down then try to get extras thrown in for free. How about trying to get a tow bar fitted or a full MoT or free delivery thrown in, all of which may represent less to the vendor, in cash terms, than to you. If you buy a project vehicle, for example, it might cost you a couple of hundred pounds to hire a trailer and fetch it, whereas the vendor might have all the gear and drop it off when passing at no extra expense to himself. Bring up such suggestions during the negotiations and not as an afterthought when the vendor thinks the negotiations are concluded, since that makes it look as if you're after a double discount.

Try to conduct the negotiations on neutral ground if you're a purchaser. Try to stay with the

ABOVE Look for other ways of getting added value in a deal such as free delivery!

RIGHT Try and avoid
comfortable chairs or
over-desk situations
that put you as a buyer
at a disadvantage

vehicle even if it's cold and wet outside. A good place to negotiate is while sitting in the vehicle at the end of a successful test drive, as with your interest in acquiring it and the vendor's in disposing of it it's a sort of shared neutral ground. Once you move away from the vehicle it becomes a transient memory rather than a solid object in direct contact with almost all of your senses. Whilst many vendors prefer to conduct their negotiations elsewhere they'd fare better if they left the potential purchaser in contact with the vehicle. If you do end up in an office or house be aware that it's putting you at a disadvantage as you're prey in their lair, and there are likely to be many distractions, especially if it's a domestic residence full of children and televisions.

Avoid all offers of hospitality until the

negotiations are over. The comfy chair, the warm room and the hot drink (or cool room and cold drink as appropriate to the season) all conspire to take the edge off your concentration just at the point where you need it most. Prehistoric instincts also dictate in such circumstances that you're the submissive party in the other's territory and this gives him the greater power. As vendor he has the greater power anyhow, as it's he who ultimately decides if the vehicle will sell at the price on the table, not you as the purchaser, even though you may think you're driving the bargain. The vendor doesn't need any more power than the minimum you can get away with allowing him. Try to avoid a desk between you and the vendor, as it's similar to a boss/employee or teacher/pupil sort of relationship and you'll be disadvantaged and possibly feel submissive. Keep the salesman in the lounge area if you have to go indoors at a dealer's: without the formal relationship across a desk you're both mutually disadvantaged.

As a vendor the opposite is true. You know the vehicle well and don't need to be in touch with it to sell it. You're more confident on your home ground and need to try to get the purchaser's guard down in the hope that he'll give you more money or let his heart rule his head. The heart works better running on coffee in cosy surroundings, so try to get the purchaser into such an environment. For some people, though, your house may not be appropriate for the initial stages of dealing, as you may feel at risk from them. Sitting in the vehicle is the best alternative.

RIGHT Loveable as
they are, not everyone
feels the same about
pets and children so
try to keep them out of
the way

Try to get other members of the family and pets to stay out of the way. You may love your dog or cat but the potential purchaser may not and may want to leave as soon as possible because of them, without buying your Land Rover. Try to be present in numbers equal to the purchasers. If the buyer has a partner with them then get yours there too, though it's better if only one of you does the actual dealing, whether buyer or seller.

Women tend to be more extreme than men when it comes to dealing and either roll over more easily or stick out for a tougher deal. If the vendor, or if their female partner, is in the former category you may get a better deal, as they signal it's time to take the money sooner. If you or your female partner is in the latter category you may find it difficult to sell your Land Rover. In almost all cases where a subsequent investigation revealed the heart ran away with the chequebook, it was a man's signature on the cheque. If selling, therefore, try to deal with the male, as they'll probably give in and pay more than the female partner. If buying, try to include the female in the loop and you'll soon be able to judge which sort she is.

Sometimes people feel disadvantaged dealing with the opposite gender. Most franchised dealerships recognise this and employ female as well as male sales staff, who are usually better at the job than many of their male colleagues. If I was buying a Land Rover from a main dealer I'd certainly prefer to deal with a female sales person, as I'd feel confident that she was good at her job.

When trying to buy or sell a Land Rover find out what methods of payment are acceptable to the vendor or purchaser, as it may influence the negotiations. Not everyone will pay in or even accept cash in the form of folding money, especially if large sums are involved, as it's actually difficult to get this out of a bank and costs quite a bit in bank charges to pay it back in again. Some vendors won't take a certified cheque or bank draft. With internet banking more common it's sometimes actually quite hard to get a bank draft without giving several days' notice. Many people don't have bank accounts that can raise or accept electronic transfers of funds. And sensible vendors will quite rightly refuse to release a vehicle until the funds are clear in their account, and that can take several days. Electronic transfers can take three working days to show in the recipient account even though the funds have left yours. If the Land Rover is of a lower value – say, less than £1,500 – and you have folding money in your pocket and a trailer outside, or some other legal way of taking it home, the immediacy of the deal can often lead to a better price.

If selling, be as accommodating as possible without opening yourself to the risk of not getting paid. There has to be an element of trust but it's usually up to the purchaser to trust the vendor to look after the vehicle and hand it over when the money is cleared in their account rather than for the vendor to trust the purchaser and let the vehicle go immediately, hoping the cheque they have is a good one and not a 'Dunlop'.

ABOVE You will not be allowed to pay for vehicles like this with actual cash in the form of paper money. It is against company policy and you will be probably investigated under the money laundering regulations

If you don't manage to conclude the deal don't just leave. Swap phone numbers or call in after both parties have had time to reconsider their positions. There's a risk, of course, that the Land Rover may change hands in the meantime, but it often happens that in the meantime the vendor's spouse suggests they ought to have accepted your offer, or a knowing friend will have pointed out that it was a bargain and you should have offered more. It's a bit of a mean trick, but sometimes a daytime phone call to the house – especially if you think the husband is at work – opening with 'I was wondering if Mr Smith had had further thoughts about accepting my offer of £X for the Land Rover?' often works, as the spouse might not have been made aware of the price and might just have been told it wasn't enough. Knowing the figures sometimes prompts them into pushing the reluctant husband into taking the money.

If the thought of dealing face to face with a stranger when buying or selling a Land Rover frightens you then get some practice. Whilst we don't tend to haggle at a supermarket checkout there are still environments where we do. Go to a car boot sale, autojumble, or car show and buy in miniature. Look for Dinky toys or similar low-cost items and practice haggling the price. You don't even have to buy the object – it's just free practice; but if you're successful in reducing the asking price from £2.50 to £1.00 the principles used and lessons learnt can be applied to dealing for a full-sized Land Rover. You learn to read body language and how far you can push people. You also learn to gauge the time to walk away or get your purse out. It's well worth spending £20 or so acquiring a dozen toys as the practice is probably more than an average car buyer will get in the whole of his car-buying life. Better to pay a pound too much for a toy Land Rover than a thousand too much for a real one. Though he's only just realising why, I force my son to do his own toy dealing, as even though he probably won't go into the motor trade the practice of learning how to bargain with people will stand him in good stead for the rest of his life.

Bidding at auction

You may never actually meet the vendor if the Land Rover is sold by auction. Here the contact you'll have is with the auctioneer. The secret of auctions is to bid as little as you need to secure the vehicle whilst staying within your price limit. When deciding this don't forget the extras such as indemnity, and sometimes a buyers' premium and VAT (if applicable to the sort of Land Rover you're buying) may be added to the final hammer price. Having decided your maximum hammer price you need to stand at the back of the hall and to one side so that you can see the auctioneer and he can see you. You can also watch the other potential purchasers.

You may have had to pre-register to bid and have been allocated a number, and either this number or the auction catalogue are good weapons to wave when you want to denote your bid to the auctioneer. Once the auctioneer has you in sight he'll often point to you if you're winning as he casts round for extra bids. If you're outbid he'll establish eye contact with you and you need to either wave again or nod clearly to make your next bid. If you're all done, shake your head emphatically from side to side as he looks at you, declining his invitation to up your bid. You can come back in again when others have slogged it out, but you'll need to wave your catalogue again to get his attention back.

Auctioneers work in two systems: one is to call out the bid achieved, so if the auctioneer is calling out, say, 'Six hundred', then when you bid it jumps to six fifty. The other way is for the auctioneer to call out the bid he's looking for: he'll say 'Looking for six fifty', so when you wave it's that price you've bid and he'll move on to the next bid he's looking for. Most car auctions use the former system, whilst auctions for houses and other expensive items tend to use the latter and antiques sales use both. The 'bid achieved' system is easier for an inexperienced person to follow, and I like it as it enables me to take control away from the rostrum by, for example, mouthing 'fifty' as I flick the catalogue, if the bidding is in hundreds, as this slows down the rate of increase. If there are two bidders this means that each round of bidding is only £100 and not £200. Early stages of bidding are usually in large increments, sometimes as much as £500 or even £1,000, until the auctioneer says 'Take 250' or something similar to indicate that he's reduced the increments. But I like to take control before he does this, in order to reduce his domination of the auction.

I would suggest not bidding until the price starts to stall, as a three-way bid doubles the incremental amounts. I like to make only one bid and try to leave it until just before the hammer falls. I'll bid more times if needed but feel I've been run up if I have to, and will stall again until just before the hammer falls. It's most satisfying to buy on your one and only bid. Listen carefully to the auctioneer, as he'll indicate if the reserve has been reached and the vehicle is therefore sold, or if the final bid is near to the reserve and so only a provisional sale. In the latter case the auction staff will subsequently contact you and the entrant to try to move both parties towards an acceptable deal and so a successful sale. I always try to avoid such situations, as sorting them out can make me miss other vehicles in the sale that might have interested me: I prefer to not go and give my details, and the £500 deposit, and explain that I want to bid on other possibilities. But if I'm still empty-handed at the end of the sale I might go to the office and see if they can broker a deal on an unsold vehicle I was interested in, even if I wasn't the highest bidder. Though they can't sell vehicles 'over the counter' before they've been through the ring it's standard practice to try to match unsold vehicles to customers after the sale. The reserve is often lower once the entrant has had a reality check by it not being met.

There's a myth that you only have to twitch at an auction to register a bid, but in reality you have to make a bold gesture to get the auctioneer's attention, though once he's made eye contact you'll only need to make small nods of the head or slight flicks of the catalogue to register subsequent bids.

You must always be careful not to bid against yourself. Though immoral and illegal it's accepted practice for some auctioneers, even at well respected venues, to take imaginary bids in order to raise a price above the reserve and then land the next genuine bidder with the vehicle. The reason I stay at the back and to one side in an auction is to check that I'm bidding against a real person and not just 'Mr Osram the light fitting on the back wall'. If you're very clever you can often teach the auctioneer a lesson by not bidding again and forcing him to knock it down to a non-existent bidder. It's nevertheless difficult to spot an auctioneer 'taking bids off the wall', and if he's clever you won't know it's happening to you!

BELOW This person is in the ideal bidding position as he is easily visible to the auctioneer from the rostrum and at the same time can see exactly what is happening in the rest of the sale room

Checking a
vehicle's status

Dodgy dealings to watch out for **108**

Just because a person has a vehicle in their possession, and possibly even a logbook in their name, doesn't mean that they're the legal owner and have a right to take your money. Land Rover products are quite a high cost compared to other vehicles so many are bought with borrowed money.

In some cases the vehicle does indeed belong to the person who has it in his possession but in others it belongs to the financing company until it's fully paid for. The finance company will sometimes let the keeper sell it (see Chapter 7) but will send a letter stating their terms and the way to proceed that's agreeable to them. It's unlikely that a vehicle over eight years old is still on finance, but it could be that an old deal went wrong and hasn't been sorted out even after that much time so it's still worth checking on one of the Legal Title databases. Most finance companies will only touch vehicles up to five years of age and for a period of three years, but it's possible to get finance on vehicles up to seven or eight years old and those that are accepted as classics. Other 'at risk' vehicles such as hire cars and some company fleet cars are often put on these databases as well, even though there's no finance on them.

The check will usually look up the details held on the other two databases – insurance write-offs (the VCAR or Vehicle Condition Alert Register) and the Stolen Register – and it's a good idea to check any age vehicle on both of these. Being on the VCAR doesn't matter as long as you're aware of the fact, and the vehicle has been repaired properly and is priced accordingly. If it turns up on the stolen register then inform the police immediately. In some rare cases it's an error resulting from it having been put on in the past and the register having not been updated, but usually it's a warning to stay well clear.

If you're buying from a franchised dealer or an auction they'll have already checked these databases and will not be selling a vehicle on the Stolen Register and will tell prospective purchasers if it's on the VCAR. If you're buying elsewhere then for peace of mind I suggest checking any Land Rover, as some independent dealers aren't too fussy about declaring VCAR-listed vehicles.

Such checks aren't entirely foolproof, as not all finance deals are listed on the electronic databases. However, as a private individual you'll usually be fine if, after checking its history thoroughly, you unwittingly buy a vehicle that's still on finance. If you're a dealer, then insurance against 'wrongful conversion' (as it's called) ought to be regarded as an essential, though expensive, part of your Motor Trade insurances. As a private individual your insurance policy won't have any cover for wrongful conversion.

Remember that an HPI or Experian check gives you no legal rights, as you'll find out if you can read the small print.

There appears to be no legal obligation for banks to register any interest (finance agreement) with any of the electronic databases. This means that although a finance company may have forgotten to register or inaccurately registered a car, as the dealer this is your hard luck. This sometimes happens with number plate changes with 'cherished transfers', as the vehicle's listed under a different registration number to the one you checked, though the databases do try to keep track of a vehicle's original identity.

A private individual who sells a car can't pass on any better title than he actually has to a motor trader. That's to say, if there's finance on it he doesn't have title to that car, the finance company does. He's unable to pass any title on. However, if a non-motor trader purchaser enters the chain and the car is sold to them before or after the dealer purchases the vehicle they'll have gained clean title and the next owner would be able to keep the car.

Although a bank or finance company would seemingly have title to a vehicle on finance the 1964 Finance Act dramatically changed the law, so that a private individual who purchased a motor vehicle in good faith would gain clean title to it even if the vehicle was subject to a finance agreement. Motor traders and anyone dealing in cars are specific exceptions and are unable to gain clean title under any circumstances. It doesn't matter that they're totally innocent. This means that if a fraudster sells a car on finance to a private individual, who acquires the car in good faith and at a proper market value, who then subsequently sells it to a motor dealer, the dealer has good title and can keep the car. However, if the same fraudster sells the car direct to a motor dealer who subsequently sells to a private individual, the private individual acquires clean title. The motor trader has sold a car he didn't have title to so is guilty of wrongful conversion and must pay the finance company the value of the car or the finance outstanding. It's then up to the trader to pursue the fraudster.

Similarly, with the VCAR register it doesn't mean if it's not listed that it has never been crashed or never been the subject of an insurance total loss claim, as not all insurance companies operate the system. Be aware too that a Land Rover may have been crashed and repaired in its life as a normal insurance claim and repair. With high value vehicles it's possible to do a lot of work before reaching the point where the sums don't add up and make a vehicle an uneconomic repair. Whilst most have been done to a good standard not all repairs are well executed, and as time goes

BELOW This vehicle is listed on the condition alert database as accident damaged, although it was early in its life and now shows little evidence (see picture opposite)

by their legacy can return to haunt a vehicle. In particular, corrosion issues that wouldn't affect a well carried out repair or original factory build can often affect a poor repair some years later.

Dodgy dealings to watch out for

Insurance write-offs

Vehicles that are comprehensively insured may become 'insurance write-offs' when damaged if the insurance company decides that the cost of repairs is greater than the value of the vehicle less the amount it will fetch as salvage. The term in no way means the vehicle isn't repairable. Its age and thus its value is the main deciding factor – for example, a not very old Defender worth, say, £20,000 would need quite a lot of damage to become a write-off and an insurance company might spend £10,000 or more on repairs if needed. On the other hand an older Defender worth just £3,500 with the same damage and the same repair cost would be declared a constructive total loss, as the repairs would cost far more than the vehicle was worth. There are other expenses to take into account as well, such as car hire, which might cost thousands of pounds. The insurance company has a duty to get out of its liability in the most economical way, and instead of paying to have the £3,500 vehicle repaired they would pay the owner its £3,500 value and sell the wreck for salvage, possibly for as little as 20 per cent of the payout figure. The net cost to them would therefore be only £2,800.

The wreck might then be sold on by the salvage company at a profit and rebuilt using second-hand parts before being returned to the road as a safe, tidy vehicle. There's no problem with this and it's perfectly legal. However, before this can happen the wreck would first be categorised as one of four types of listed insurance write-off known as A to D, with D being the least damaged. Of these, groups A and B are required to be broken up for spare parts, group C has to undergo a vehicle identity check by the Vehicle Operator Services Agency (VOSA) at a goods vehicle test centre which is then noted on its V5C registration document, and group D can be rebuilt and returned to the road with no other check or marker on its V5C.

Groups C and D are both recorded on a database, and when a prospective purchaser does a check on the vehicle's status it will show up as a write-off. There's no compulsion for the vendor to tell you, though if asked if the vehicle is a write-off he must answer truthfully. Though the vehicle may be perfect it will never be worth the same as an undamaged one and the prospective owner needs to be aware of it. There's nothing wrong in buying a write-off as long as it's been repaired properly and is safe and the purchaser is aware of its history. Some are good value for money, especially 'stolen recovered' vehicles (group E – see next paragraph) that may have never been damaged at all or only suffered lock damage, and you ought to get a good vehicle at a low price. But it's a good idea to check the write-off status of all vehicles before purchase.

A final group known as E covers very light damage or no damage at all and is usually applied to recovered stolen vehicles. These won't show up on the database as there's nothing wrong with them, so to all intents and purposes this category doesn't exist!

Ringers

The practice of 'repairing' a vehicle by stealing a similar one and applying the identity of the crashed one to it is called 'ringing' (from the expression 'ringing the changes'). Though this is becoming more difficult on recent Land Rovers, which are now given more identifying marks during manufacture, you should still check the chassis number etc for signs of tampering. However, the practice remains common with older Land Rovers, especially those purporting to be pre-1973 Series vehicles, and Range Rovers which have had older identities applied to either genuine or stolen vehicles to make them free of road tax and so cheaper to run.

Though no amount of register checking will make you aware that such vehicles aren't as described, their colour and the presence of later features than expected for their age can provide a clue. For example, I recently looked at a Range Rover purporting to be a genuine 1972 model, but its colour, Sand Glow, was only used between 1975–9 and was all over the inside as original. The chassis number also proved to be unreadable, so I left that one where it was. Another was a '1971' Series III 88 but it had the later style rear lights, twin circuit servo brakes, and other features suggesting that it was actually a 1983 vehicle, or newer, on an older logbook. In both cases I don't think the current owner was the one who actually did it, but several owners and years later it's difficult to sort out, so that one I also left alone. I recently saw a '1972' tax-exempt 101 for sale on eBay, but its date of registration was too early for a 101, of which only about 20 were built in 1972. The vendor wouldn't give me the chassis number to check but I bet it was from a normal vehicle and this ringer 101 was either stolen or just disguised to save a previous owner some money.

Unfortunately, this sort of intimate product knowledge is difficult to gain and it's hard to find someone with such experience to look at vehicles. It's therefore important that you try to swat up on the features expected on the specific vehicle you're proposing to buy. Be especially vigilant with 1971–2 Series III Land Rovers and 1970–2 Range Rovers claiming 'free road tax status'. If in doubt, the technical officers of the various clubs applicable to your model of Land Rover will often help and their current contact details are usually found as listings in publications such as *Land Rover Monthly*.

Clones

A 'clone' results from the practice of stealing a vehicle, applying the identity of a similar vehicle to it by means of false or stolen number plates and forged paperwork, and then selling it. In effect there are then two vehicles in existence with exactly the same identity but only one is genuine. Though the clone may look fine on a vehicle status check if the original has no problems, it's nevertheless a stolen vehicle and when it all comes out you'll lose it and your money, as you never had legal title. It's not that widespread a practice since on the whole only high value vehicles justify the risk and investment in the forged paperwork etc. Recent measures such as a VIN number etched behind the windscreen and

ABOVE This 1983 onwards split lighting arrangement should not be seen on older vehicles, especially those claiming free road tax status

LEFT Easily visible VIN numbers were introduced to reduce cloning and ringing of vehicles

anti-forging features in the registration document
have led to a decline in cloning, but it's still
necessary to apply due diligence to your checking
process – not least because clones are usually
offered at low prices so that the thrill of getting a
bargain overrides your natural caution. Just be
aware that if something's too good to be true it
probably isn't!

Theft

Potential purchasers may not be anything of the
sort and are actually trying to get hold of your
Land Rover without paying for it. They may be
intending to do this by way of forged bank drafts,
forged cash, or forged building society cheques,
or by gaining control on a test drive and driving
off. With ever more sophisticated security
measures being built into vehicles, such tricks are
utilised because the keys are now usually needed
before they can be taken. However, this sort of
theft is more prevalent with high value vehicles, as
the risk isn't justified on a cheap vehicle.

When showing your vehicle to a buyer you
need to be aware that such things can happen
and do as much as possible to protect yourself
and your property. However, don't be paranoid to
the point of scaring off a genuine purchaser. If you
feel vulnerable then consider selling your Land
Rover in another environment, such as an auction,
or have a 'minder' with you when a pre-arranged
inspection takes place. Don't take everybody at
face value and be especially wary of anyone
appearing to look at your vehicle with several
'helpers', especially if two of them want to go with
you on the test drive and the rest want to stay
behind. Their plan may be to rob your house while
you're away. If the others then push you out of

your Land Rover somewhere isolated and drive
away you may even find that under such
circumstances its loss isn't covered by your
insurance policy.

Money scams

Trying to obtain a vehicle without paying is now
becoming a more common way of stealing a
vehicle. One method is to 'buy' your vehicle with a
stolen bank draft or cheque. You release the
vehicle and only find out later that the money isn't
forthcoming. Another scam is for a buyer to
telephone you, ostensibly from abroad, and send
you a cheque drawn on a foreign, often Nigerian,
bank. It seemingly clears in your bank and you
release the vehicle to the purchaser's 'cousin'.
Because of the delays in international banking it
may take weeks before the cheque is eventually
bounced by the issuing bank, upon which your
own bank will retrieve the funds from your account
and you're left with no money and no vehicle. To
add insult to injury the trickster often includes the
'shipping costs' in his payment and asks you to
draw these in cash to give to the 'cousin' when he
collects the vehicle. They also usually give the
asking price in order to make as much as they
can out of the fraud.

It all sounds very plausible because these are,
after all, professional con artists. Once again you'll
usually find that you're not insured against losing a
vehicle in circumstances like these, so only
release it when you're absolutely certain the
money is genuine. People really do buy from
abroad, but an electronic transfer is best for such
transactions as it takes three working days at
most for these to appear in your bank as
guaranteed funds.

Finance

A private individual may try to sell a car that's still
on finance. They may genuinely have permission
from the legal owner – ie the finance company –
and that's fine, and you might be asked to make
two payments, the settlement figure to the finance
company and the balance to the keeper. This is all
fine and proper, if a little tiresome to do. On the
other hand you might be deliberately deceived into
unwittingly buying a vehicle that's subject to
finance. Often it's a bogus person who 'owns' it,
or sometimes a real person about to do a runner.
Almost no amount of checking will alert you to this
but if you paid the market rate and bought as a
private individual you ought to be safe. It's one of
the risks associated with a private purchase and
the reason why you need to do a check on the
vehicle before handing over the funds.

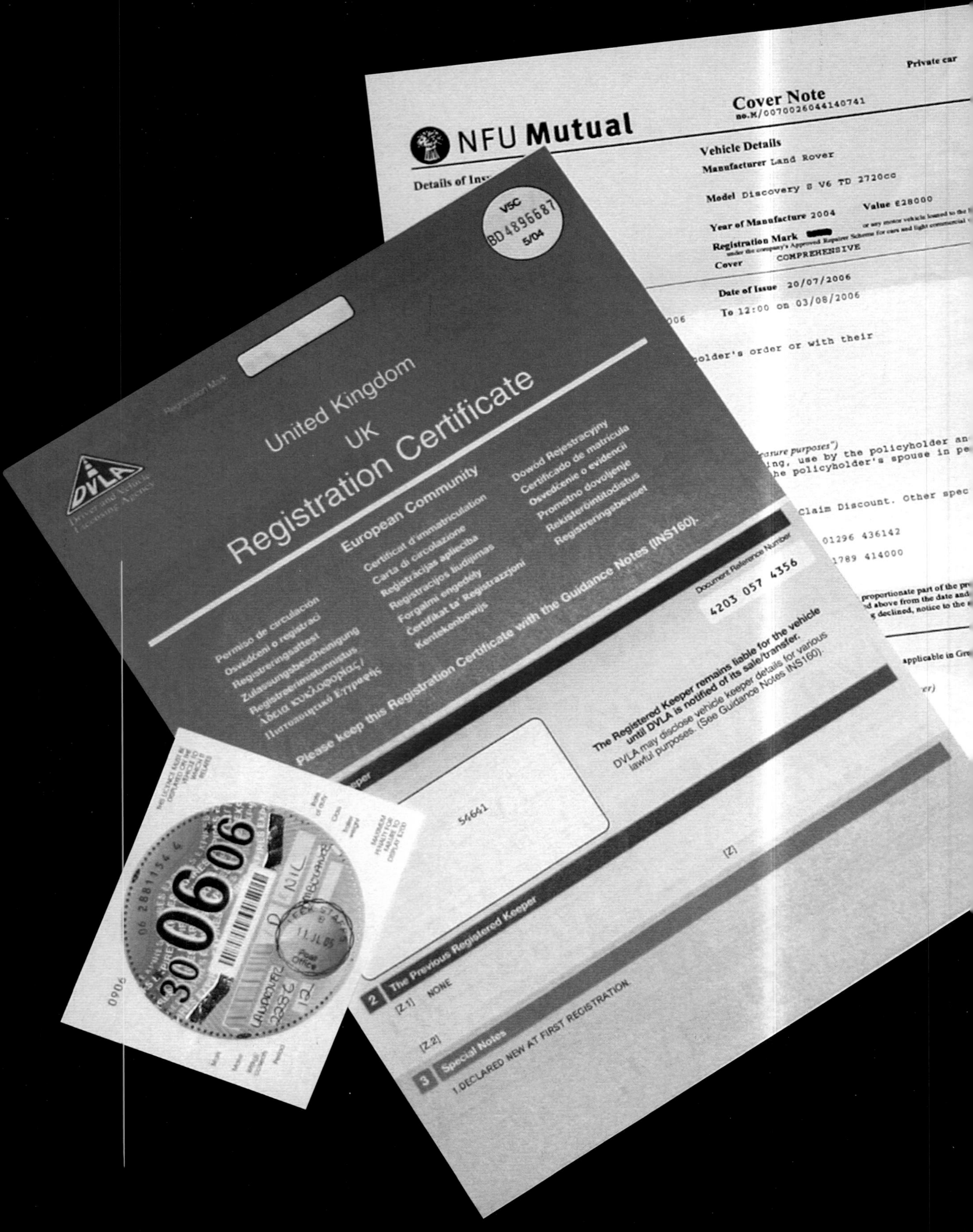

VSC
BD4896687
5/04

Registration Mark

United Kingdom
UK
Registration Certificate

European Community

Dowód Rejestracyjny
Certificado de matricula
Osvedčenie o evidencii
Prometno dovoljenje
Rekisteröintitodistus
Registreringsbevisett

Certificat d'immatriculation
Carta di circolazione
Registrācijas apliecība
Registracijos liudijimas
Forgalmi engedély
Certifikat ta' Reġistrazzjoni
Kentekenbewijs

Permiso de circulacion
Osvedčeni o registraci
Registreringsattest
Zulassungsbescheinigung
Registrərimistunnistus
Άδεια κυκλοφορίας/
Πιστοποιητικό Εγγραφής

Please keep this Registration Certificate with the Guidance Notes (INS160).

Document Reference Number

4203 057 4356

**The Registered Keeper remains liable for the vehicle
until DVLA is notified of its sale/transfer.**
DVLA may disclose vehicle keeper details for various
lawful purposes. (See Guidance Notes INS160).

[Z]

54641

2 The Previous Registered Keeper

[Z1] NONE

[Z2]

3 Special Notes

1.DECLARED NEW AT FIRST REGISTRATION

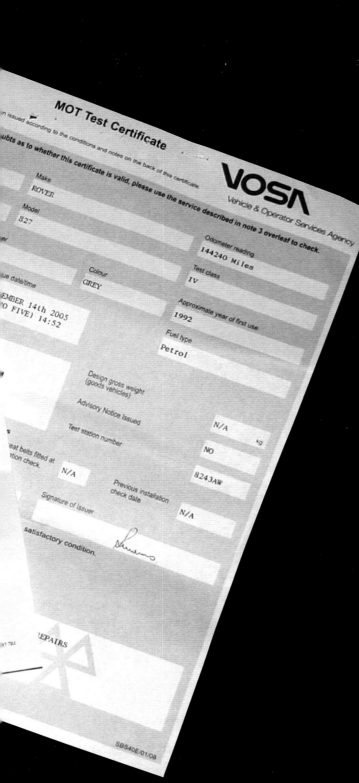

Getting the paperwork in order

MoT, tax and insurance

To legally drive a motor vehicle on the public road you need three items to be valid: MoT, road tax and insurance.

The MoT certificate needs to be in force for all Land Rovers over three years of age. It's possible to drive a vehicle to and from a previously arranged test within a reasonable distance from your home. It's also legal to drive from an MoT station to a garage or workshop for repairs following a failure. This doesn't give you an excuse to drive a project vehicle home by booking it in for a test at the garage nearest to your house, possibly hundreds of miles away.

There needs to be a valid tax disc for the vehicle and it needs to be displayed in the front nearside of the windscreen. You may, however, drive to and from a previously arranged MoT test without displaying a tax disc or having a valid one in force. If you have an insurance certificate for the vehicle, or it's on the insurance database as being insured by you, then it's possible to purchase a tax disc at most Post Offices in working hours.

You need to have a minimum of third party insurance cover for any vehicle you drive on the road. This is the legal minimum and covers you for the costs of claims made against you in the event of an accident. It's called 'third party' because the claimant is the third party in the proceedings with you and your insurance company the first and second parties respectively. The next level of cover is 'third party fire and theft'. This covers you for third party claims made against you, and if your Land Rover is stolen or catches fire you'll be reimbursed for the value of it. The next level of insurance is fully comprehensive. This will cover the cost of repairs to your vehicle even if the damage is your fault, as well as for fire, theft, and any third party claim.

Fully comprehensive often includes extras such as legal expense cover as well, so that if you make a claim against another party, following an accident for which you aren't to blame, the legal expenses will be covered in the event of not being able to recover them from the person who caused the accident or their insurance company. In a 'non blame' accident you may well be covered for the cost of a hire vehicle whilst yours is being repaired or the claim settled.

Insurance is specific to a vehicle and will cover a limited number of drivers. They may be named, above a certain age, or indeed be any driver. In some instances the insurance will cover the policy holder to drive another vehicle not belonging to them with third party cover. This is now getting rarer but was designed for emergency use if you suddenly found you needed to drive another person's car. It won't cover you to drive a recent purchase home, as you own it even if the V5C doesn't list you as the owner. You can't drive it home on the previous owner's insurance either, and they probably won't be covered to deliver it as they don't legally own it any more. You therefore need to arrange proper cover, and usually if you use a broker they can do it over the telephone, thereby covering you to drive home legally provided the vehicle is taxed and has an MoT.

Though you might not be caught it's not advisable to drive with no tax or MoT, but with insurance, MoT, and Road Tax details now on databases it's increasingly likely you'll be clocked by one of the fixed roadside cameras with a number plate recognition facility, and so risk a fine arriving in the post. However, never, *ever* risk driving with no insurance cover, as it's an utterly irresponsible thing to do. If you're so desperate to get your new acquisition home, then pay to have it shifted on a trailer or lorry, or leave it until you can get the proper cover and other paperwork in order. The costs will be cheaper than the fine.

Test drives are another area of risk. You're usually covered by a dealer's insurance to test-drive one of their vehicles, though usually they'll need to see your driving licence and possibly photocopy it for their files, and you'll usually need to be accompanied by one of their staff to validate the insurance and to stop you driving off in it. You're unlikely to be covered at a private venue, though if the owner has full cover for any driver you may be. It might be safest to let the owner drive anyway, as even if you're covered under your own policy for other vehicles it's usually the legal minimum and if you damage the test vehicle you'll be personally responsible. Watch owners carefully, though, to check they're not concealing any faults by their driving style!

Motor dealers and traders and some private collectors have what's called a 'Trade' policy, which covers them to drive other cars. The cover may be third party or comprehensive but covers

ABOVE The modern computerised test system means fake test certificates are easily detected

OPPOSITE Unless going to and returning from a pre-arranged MoT test you need a valid tax disc to drive on UK roads. There are no excuses so don't risk it

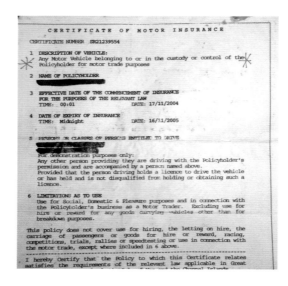

them to drive 'any vehicle the property of the
policyholder or in their care custody or control',
and if you're selling a vehicle they may want to
test-drive it on their insurance. Don't just take their
word they're covered: you need to see the actual
policy and even jot down the details of the
company and policy number. If your vehicle is
worth more than a few hundred pounds then they
need to have fully comprehensive cover, as third
party won't cover your vehicle if they were to
damage it.

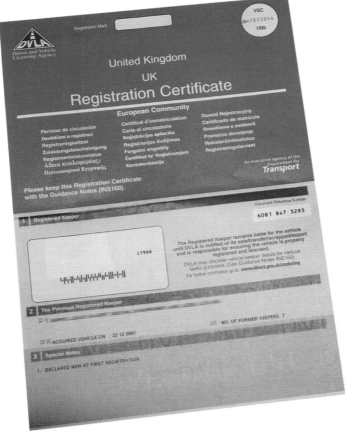

The Logbook (V5C)

The main document that accompanies a vehicle is
the Registration Certificate or V5C. It's commonly
called the 'logbook', a throwback to pre-computer
days when each vehicle had its own card logbook
that accompanied it throughout its life, in which
changes of ownership were recorded. In the late
1970s a big computer system was built at
Swansea because it was an area of high
unemployment and eligible for funding under a
scheme to provide employment. All the paper
records held by the various county registration
authorities were then transferred to the database
at Swansea and computer-printed registration
documents replaced the old card logbooks. Since
then the V5 registration document has itself
undergone several changes, the most recent
being in 2005 when it was redesigned to be
similar to documents used in the rest of Europe.

All vehicles currently in use ought to have the
current V5C or one of the tear-off sections from it.
Older 'barn finds' and project vehicles may not
have current paperwork, and reclaiming the
original number may be one of the costs and
processes the new owner has to go through to
get the vehicle back on the road.

The current V5C has a lot of information about
both the vendor and the vehicle and ought to be
studied intently. It's inner sections 4 and 5 that
we're most interested in, as they contain
information that the vendor can verify. Of
course, if the vehicle is for sale at a dealer the
details aren't as important to verify as in a private
sale environment.

Section 5 gives details of the registered keeper
(not necessarily the legal owner), which ought to be
the same person as the one who's selling the
vehicle, at the address where you're looking at it. If
it's not, ascertain who the person in the V5C is and
possibly even get their telephone number to confirm
that the vendor has permission to sell it before you
continue with the deal. There are many explanations
that may be valid, such as 'on behalf of a friend' or
'it's a relative's vehicle', but it could just as easily be
a dealer in disguise and you should be wary.

The next thing is the date of acquisition. Does it
confirm the answer to the casual question as to
how long they've owned it? Section 2 has the
previous keeper and when it was bought, so if the
current vendor claims to have bought it in, say,
Brighton whereas the previous owner is listed as
being in Aberdeen it may give you cause to doubt
the validity of anything else they say.

Section 4 has all the vehicle details and these

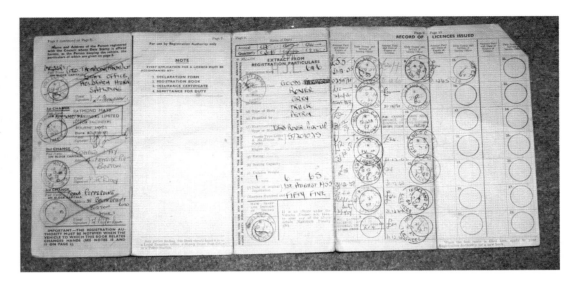

LEFT This is a logbook, and is where the term comes from, but is of no legal use whatsoever other than in the history file of a classic vehicle as its legal status finished in the seventies

need to be confirmed against the vehicle itself. Some may be wrong, such as engine number if it has not been amended when repair work has been carried out, but the VIN or Vehicle Identity Number needs to be the same as is displayed on the vehicle. The colour ought to be right as well, though if it's had a colour change and not been amended in the V5C traces of the old colour as listed will possibly be found under the bonnet. The colour details are only basic and the vehicle may be 'Copperleaf Bronze' in the advert but 'Brown' on the V5C. If you're selling a vehicle try to make certain the details are correct before you offer it for sale, and get them amended if wrong so as not to preclude a sale.

When you complete a purchase the vendor will send the V5C off with your details in it and you'll receive a replacement in the post. You ought to be given the Section 10, as it acts as a temporary registration certificate lasting two months or until the full one arrives. If you sell to a dealer, auction house, or insurance company they'll want the whole document, but detach Section 9 and send it to the DVLA, informing them of the transfer so that they can address any issues such as non-declaration of SORN (Statutory Off Road Notification) or even speeding tickets to the relevant party.

There are full instructions on what to do with the paperwork when you buy and sell vehicles, so it may pay to study the back of your current vehicle's document to learn how to proceed in the forthcoming transaction.

Due to delays in receiving the V5C vehicles may be offered for sale without the full registration certificate. If this is the case the vendor ought to at least have the Section 10 portion and, ideally, a photocopy of the original. You need to at least have Section 10 if not the full document to be able to tax a vehicle, so if it's not taxed and you don't have these you may have to wait six weeks or more before you can drive it. This doesn't matter if it's a long-term project but it is a bit frustrating to have an untaxed £25K Range Rover sitting on the drive for six weeks while you wait for the paperwork to catch up.

The V5C is often missing where the vehicle has had a 'cherished number' transferred to a replacement, so be warned – especially if there's less than two months' tax on the windscreen – that you may not be able to tax it again if the paperwork isn't present.

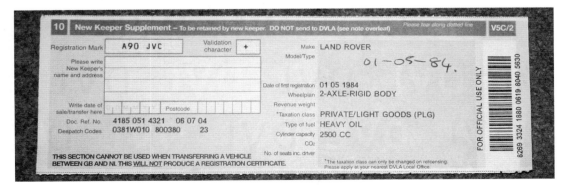

LEFT If the full V5C is not available (it may still be on a return journey from DVLA) then the vendor should have section 10 and this is the only bit you initially receive when the vehicle becomes your property

Checking it physically

There are three ways of physically checking a Land Rover. One is a methodical approach, starting with one of the various systems on the vehicle and then moving on to another, such as the engine and then the interior. The next method is to start at one point and check everything in the area, such as by starting at one front corner and checking the tyre and wheel, then the chassis and axle and then the inner wing and lights all in the same area before moving to another location. The third method – and this is the preferred way – is to initially target the most likely generic problems for that model of Land Rover and, if they're all OK, move on to a general inspection.

It's pointless spending time looking at a vehicle if that particular model's known weak points aren't right. On a Discovery Series 1, for example, the rear floor under the carpet, the sills, and the front inner wings are well-known corrosion points and the most likely reason not to buy so start there. The gearbox is also known to be weak, so if the corrosion isn't present or is at an acceptable level for the price then check the gearbox (without moving the vehicle) for a clunk when taking up drive. If you still can't find a reason not to buy then move on to a proper full inspection and a road test if possible.

On a Series Land Rover chassis and bulkhead corrosion are the main reasons for keeping your money in your pocket, so look at the chassis first and if that's passable the bulkhead, before giving the rest of it a check.

Each item should be inspected for three reasons: for safety and legality, for problems in

LEFT Target known problem areas such as the rear body crossmember on this Discovery

need of immediate attention, and for the onset of a problem that will require attention at a future date. A bald tyre, for example, is unsafe and illegal; a slipping clutch will need immediate attention; and scabby rust on an inner wing will probably mean it's been perforated and will need a welding repair when the next MoT is due. It's a non-dismantling and non-destructive examination, though a small jack is needed to check the suspension.

You need either to know exactly what makes a Land Rover tick or else get someone who does to carry out the inspection. It needn't be a specialist from the motoring organisations, just a knowledgeable person who's possibly a friend. Unfortunately these are hard to come by and you'll probably need to use the services of the specialist inspection companies. These charge anywhere from £100–£300 but in relation to some of the screen prices it's not a lot to pay for peace of mind. An RAC full inspection including status check is at the top end of the scale, but if you were buying a £15,000 vehicle from a dealer or private individual it would only represent 2 per cent of the value. Whether you got the seller to fix the problems before purchase or decided to walk away from a potential money pit, either way the inspection would have been good value, as it would be even if the vehicle got a clean bill of health.

The difficult vehicles are the ones from, say, £1,500 upwards where the cost of the inspection is significant and there's a great chance of the report causing you not to continue with the purchase. I'd suggest a more informal inspection is best, with the examiner taking fair wear and tear into account. If you rely on friends they need to be genuinely knowledgeable and not just enthusiasts.

Though you can probably rely on their judgement you have no legal redress if they miss something. Cheaper Land Rovers will almost certainly have problems and are usually bought and run by people who do their own work and can assess the viability of the purchase for themselves. A motor engineer or mechanic in the old meaning of the term is possibly a reasonable person to use, though a fitter isn't, as a lifetime of fitting exhausts doesn't provide enough experience to qualify someone to offer advice on a prospective purchase.

The best method is to satisfy yourself that the major insurmountable problems specific to a particular model of Land Rover, such as floor rot in a Discovery 1, aren't present, and then move on to a methodical inspection.

BELOW As the price rises it may be worth having an independent inspection by either a specialist or one of the motoring organisations

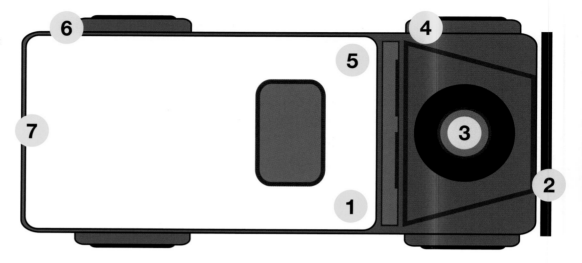

RIGHT All full
inspections should start
from the driver's seat
and end there again

Start by sitting in the driver's seat. Check all the
controls and warning lights for function. Check the
door itself for window operation and corrosion and
move on to the sill area. Then move to the front
inner wing and suspension and wheel assembly.

Move to the front and check the headlight for
cracks and corrosion and then to the engine.
Look for leaks and obvious problems.

See what sort of state the oil is in on the
dipstick and then check the radiator and look at
the antifreeze. Move to the nearside headlight and
then on to the nearside inner wing.

The wheel and suspension are next, before the
door and sill. Sit inside and check the door and
seat and window.

The sill check continues to the rear nearside
door. Check the door for corrosion and the
window for operation and the body and seatbelt
mount for corrosion. Move to the rear wheel
assembly and chassis and on to the rear via the
rear light.

Check the door for operation, and the inside
floor if not already checked, and the spare wheel.

Look at the fuel tank and chassis, especially if
a tow bar is fitted.

Move round to the offside wheel assembly via
the rear light and then on to the door and sill
before ending at the driver's seat again.

Now start the engine and listen for noises. Go
to the engine and check for excess fuming from
the oil filler and anything else untoward. Now shut
the bonnet and road test it if allowed to do so by
the vendor and if it's insured and taxed etc. Check
for clutch bite point and gear operations. Check
that the steering works and it all drives properly.

2

3

4

5

6

7

RIGHT Looking underneath will reveal a lot more about a vehicle than a surface inspection. This one looks tidy and even has traces of oil near the level plug, confirming a recent service as claimed by the vendor

RIGHT Alloy wheels look nice but are much more prone to damage, especially on working vehicles. They are also prone to kerb scuffing and corrosion so inspect them carefully

Check the brakes and look for signs of overheating and warning lights. Then return to base. If the tester is familiar with the model he'll have a mental picture of how they usually drive and can compare this specific vehicle with his experience of them, but if not he can just see if it drives as it ought to.

List any problems according to severity, but bear in mind that the vehicle is a used one and expect it to display a degree of wear and tear. The extent, though, should be consistent with the age, declared mileage, and cost of the vehicle in question. All too often potential purchasers are disappointed, as they're looking for an 'as new' second-hand vehicle, and such things just don't exist. The expectations of the purchaser need to be in tune with reality, so never expect more from a

vehicle than one could reasonably expect it to offer.

When the inspection has been completed discuss your findings with the vendor. It's unlikely your check sheet will be clean so you'll have to decide how the problems are going to be dealt with. This is a 'go, no go' point and you'll have to decide if the problems you've found will form the basis of an offer or if you'll be leaving the vehicle where it is.

Tow bars and towing

With the exception of the Freelander all recent Land Rover products have an authorised towing limit of 3.5 tons on the road with a braked trailer using the overrun system. This increases to 4 tons with a suitable hitch if the tow vehicle and trailer are fitted with a full air, vacuum, or electric braking system. The Freelander has a 2-ton limit and the Series Land Rovers have various limits depending on the year of manufacture. Many Land Rover vehicles are bought for towing duties, from small box trailers and caravans to big trailers running at the maximum 3.5 tons gross.

The cost of fitting a tow bar and wiring can be quite high and it's often a bonus to find one already fitted to a potential purchase. If the vehicle has only been used to tow a box trailer to the rubbish tip every couple of weeks then this is indeed a bonus, but if it's been towing a 3.5-ton mini-digger around for 39,500 of its 40,000 miles then it will obviously be pretty worn. It's therefore best to try to buy a vehicle without a tow bar fitted and without the telltale signs of one having been removed.

As it's quite difficult to find a Land Rover without one, especially among the more commercial types, you need to inspect the tow bar set-up for signs of wear and if possible make enquiries about its use. The tow ball will wear on the face between the ball and the vehicle, as this is where the load point is. The back face wears as well but to a lesser degree. If the plating of the ball has all gone and it looks worn and horrible then the vehicle has probably done some hard work in its past life and this should be factored into the value. As far as 90s, 110s, and Defenders are concerned they're commercial vehicles and it's rare that they've not been used for towing, so this sort of usage is considered normal for them and the value allows for this. If these types of Land Rover have not been used for towing in a past life then that really is a rare bonus.

Diesel and LPG conversions

Land Rover products tend to use more fuel than the average car and right from the early days various diesel conversions were on offer from outside manufacturers. In more recent times the readily available Rover V8 engine has led to many older vehicles being fitted with one of these in place of their old low-powered four-cylinder engine. Range Rovers were initially only available with a petrol V8 engine but many have since been retro-fitted with one of more than 100 different sorts of diesel. Some of these will have been new when fitted but many had already seen service in a small lorry or van.

I'd advise you to avoid any vehicle that doesn't have its original engine for several reasons:

- The engine may be obsolete and spares difficult to find – even if it's a common engine the adapted items, such as exhaust pipe and hoses, may be difficult to get hold of.
- The quality of the conversion job is often poor.
- If the suspension, brakes, and other systems aren't upgraded as necessary the vehicle may be dangerous to use.
- It's quite difficult and often expensive to get proper insurance cover for non-standard vehicles.
- And whilst the conversion may do more miles to the gallon it's the overall running costs you have to look at, and it may be cheaper to run the original engine.

LEFT This tow ball is well worn on the front face and the two sides and is typical of one that has done quite a lot of trailer work. Whilst expected on Land Rover vehicles, it may point towards a hard previous life

The only conversion I'd consider is a Land Rover TDI engine, especially if it was one of Land Rover's own retro-fit kits that included everything to bring the vehicle up to the then-current production standard, because insurance companies will regard this as a standard vehicle and spares are readily available.

Liquid petroleum gas conversions are another way of getting further for your money. They're potentially dangerous, of course, so properly fitted systems come with a certificate to say they've been correctly installed. Many, though, are fitted by home mechanics and may be unsafe to use. If you buy a vehicle converted to LPG the certificate needs to be present so that you can show it to your insurance company and get proper cover. If you don't tell them it's been converted there's a risk that they won't cover you in the event of a claim.

BELOW Perkins 4.203 engines like this should be avoided along with most other diesel conversions

What to look for

Series Land Rovers (1948–85)

There were three distinct series of these vehicles – Series I, which ran from 1948 to 1958, followed by Series II up to 1971, and Series III from 1971 to the end of manufacture. These can all be clearly identified by their suspension, which consisted of semi-elliptical leaf-springs at each corner. Each series was quite individual but shared a lot of components with, and was really just an improvement and upgrade of, the previous model. From a buying point of view they all tend to have the same strengths and weaknesses so can be regarded as one group.

The Series Land Rover was once the mainstay of British industry and agriculture and all branches of the services ran big fleets of them, but those in the UK have mostly been retired now and the remaining stock is in the hands of enthusiasts and other private users. However, in some less fortunate parts of the world, especially Third World countries, they're still the mainstay 4x4 and continue to work hard for a living.

There are three main areas to look at when inspecting a Series Land Rover, and it's probably best to cover these before doing a full examination.

Corrosion is the biggest issue and the hardest and most expensive to deal with. Whilst many repair sections are available, and even new chassis and bulkheads, the cost of such components and the time spent doing the work

LEFT The earliest Land Rovers were 80-inch wheelbase such as this 1952 model and many are still in working order, though unrestored

LEFT Series II from late fifties still in everyday use

BELOW Not all Land Rovers are made in the UK. These were built in Spain by Santana

will almost certainly be greater than the value of the vehicle. It's therefore much better financially to buy one with little or no rust than to buy a project. Finances aside, though, it's very rewarding to buy a Land Rover that's down and restore it back to good health, and the investment will be repaid by many years of duty rather than by trying to turn a profit at the end of the job.

The chassis is the main area to look at. You need to check that there are no areas of latent corrosion and that any previous repair work has been carried out to a satisfactory standard. The rear crossmember on all models is a favourite place to start, with the protruding outriggers and main rails next. Use a very small hammer or metal object such as a spanner. Tapping the chassis in good areas will give a metallic ringing noise. Corrosion or poor areas will give a dull thud and you might even penetrate through. Once you've found corrosion there's no need to poke big holes everywhere as it's not your property, so if you do find or make holes then tell the vendor straight away and either leave the vehicle alone or negotiate the price on that basis.

Always be wary of freshly applied bituminous underseal. It may be there as a genuine rust preventative or it may be there to a cover up poor material or workmanship.

The bulkhead is another notorious rust area, in the footwells and at the top around the screen mounts. It's possible to repair with new sections, but again, the cost of a new one and its replacement is probably more than the vehicle is worth.

The drivetrain of Series vehicles is usually not much of a problem. Front axles do corrode on the swivel housings but can be rebuilt quite cheaply. Springs sag and corrode and the gearboxes get a

bit clunky and jump out of gear. All the standard engines are quite reliable and have no special problems to look out for.

If you intend to buy a Series vehicle as a collectable item that will hopefully appreciate then beware of non-original fittings. It was common practice to fit later engines, gearboxes, and axles into Series I and II Land Rovers when the originals wore out. It was also normal to upgrade the lighting system and other electrical items, and even the brakes may be from a later model. These modifications are no problem if you just want to run the vehicle but are often difficult and expensive to return to original and ought to significantly depress the value.

All Series I and II Land Rovers are exempt from Road Tax in the UK, as are Series III built before the end of 1972. As mentioned earlier, this saving has prompted the practice of using the registration details of older vehicles on more recent ones to save the cost of paying tax. If, therefore, you're looking at a vehicle claiming to be a pre-1973 Series III make certain the vehicle is the one described in the paperwork and not a 'ringer' using the paperwork of an older, scrapped vehicle.

The 101 (1972–8) and Lightweight (1968–85)

There are several military versions of the basic Series vehicles. These come in various forms, from conventional-looking vehicles, often with heavy-duty components and specialised 24v charging systems, to the Lightweight, essentially a standard short wheelbase with special minimalist bodywork, and the 101, a very small-volume bespoke vehicle that shares many components with other Land Rover products but has numerous bits that are unique and may now be difficult and expensive to obtain.

Unless you're enthused by the military origins of such vehicles they're best left alone, as their complexity makes for greater running costs. They also tend to be sold at quite a price premium over standard vehicles, which might be worth paying to get the right vehicle if you're a military enthusiast, but aren't if you're an average buyer wanting a straightforward vehicle.

This price structuring is a carry-over from the days when military vehicles were sold off after little use and were a quality product worth more than an equivalent civilian vehicle. Now, though, the military dealers are offering vehicles that aren't built to the same standard as their civilian counterparts, in that they have sliding-window doors, no power steering, and older style normally aspirated diesel engines that have seen hard use, with possibly a couple of desert wars behind them. Unless you want them because you're a military enthusiast

they're not worth the extra money and ought to fetch less than a civilian vehicle.

A 101 or Lightweight will invariably be ex-military, as they were only produced for this market. If you want one, they've all been sold out of service and are in the hands of specialist dealers and enthusiasts. The Lightweight appeals to off-roaders as well as to military enthusiasts and fetches much more money than an equivalent civilian Series II or III, but you should only buy one if it appeals to you and you're happy to pay the premium. Some parts, including most of the running gear, are really cheap, but the specialist bodywork – in particular the bulkhead top piece – is almost impossible to find new and is expensive second-hand.

The 101 is a specialist vehicle and not really a practical everyday machine. If you want one of these superb off-road Land Rovers then you need to be prepared to pay big money, and at 16mpg fuel will be expensive. Some spares are hard to find and expensive. If you can afford to live with such difficulties then you'll have a vehicle that's not depreciating and will be a very rewarding experience to own.

BELOW The 101 and Lightweight were only ever sold to the military, so all on sale now have a former service life

90/110 Land Rovers (1983–9)

ABOVE 110 Land Rover from 1983 had not changed much visually from earlier models. The suspension was much improved though

The Land Rover 110 was introduced in early 1983 as a replacement for the Series III, and was joined in 1984 by the shorter wheelbase 90 model. Featuring many improvements over their predecessors, the coil-spring suspension, disc front brakes, and optional power steering really brought these vehicles up to date. Much of this comprised tried and tested engineering, as 13 years of Range Rover production – from where many of the new parts originated – had already proved these components. There were improvements to the engines and gearboxes as well, including permanent four-wheel drive. However, the body style was virtually unchanged except for wheel spats to cover the wider axles

and a taller front windscreen. The 110 initially retained sliding side-windows but took on the wind-up type when the 90 was introduced.

Available with either four-cylinder petrol or diesel engines, they were initially a bit underpowered at 2.25 litres, though that couldn't be said of the 3.5-litre V8 110 and the later 90. The engines were soon up to 2.5 litres and the diesel became available as a turbo unit, though it wasn't especially reliable in this form.

Available as Pick Ups, Hard Tops, full soft tops and station wagons, there's a body style to suit most people. The 110 was also available as a high capacity Pick Up with a much bigger payload area. The call for even more space led to the

RIGHT AND FAR RIGHT Sliding windows lasted until 1984 when the 90 was brought out with drop down glass

development of an even longer wheelbase 127. With the biggest allowable gross weight of any Land Rover at 3,500kg and capable of pulling a 3,500kg trailer, this was mainly used by utility companies and the military.

Available until 1989, various improvements were incorporated in the 90/110 over the years, including push-button door handles and a smoother roof. But some 'improvements', such as giving up the galvanising of some steel body parts and the front bumper, were retrogressive steps.

The 110 is at its best with the V8 engine, though unless running on LPG there's a fuel cost penalty. The 2.5 diesels are sluggish and need the rubber timing belt replaced at regular intervals.

However, the major issue with the 90/110 is corrosion, which is commonplace in the chassis, especially on the rear and protruding outriggers. The steel front bulkhead rusts, as does the rear body frame on the five-door station wagon. Rust on the bulkhead shows first in the top corners below the windscreen fixing points and then in the footwells, with the top rail being last to succumb. The doorframes corrode too, and so does the body capping on the later models. But they're good vehicles if you can find an unrusted one, as they don't have all the complicated electronics and computer control of the engine to give trouble.

The turbo diesel is a nice unit when working but it's prone to cylinder head cracking, block

ABOVE The last of the 90/110 and in this case 127 progressed to push button door handles as well

LEFT Corrosion of the steel bulkhead is another problem, though easily spotted

FAR LEFT Rubber timing belt failure is a big problem on 1984–1989 diesel powered Land Rovers

cracking, and piston-melting problems. The non-turbo diesels are much more reliable, but I'd only contemplate one in a 90, as they aren't over-blessed with power and can struggle a bit with a full load. The LT77 gearboxes suffer selection problems with age and the mainshaft wears at the rear until all drive is lost. The V8 was fitted with a five-speed Santana gearbox for a while which, though really strong, suffers layshaft bearing problems, characterised by a whine in first, second, third, and fifth gears. Earlier V8 engines had the old Range Rover four-speed gearbox, which is very reliable and long lasting. The power steering is great but it's prone to oil leaks and the axles can get rusty cases and leak. The front chrome swivels are also prone to rust. The clutch arm can punch through on its fulcrum and you're unlikely to spot it before it happens.

Though cumulatively this sounds horrific most vehicles aren't suffering from all of these problems, and virtually everything is available to fix them, whether new, OE, or second-hand. The 90/110 is inexpensive to buy, is a bit more user-friendly than the older models, and isn't as expensive to maintain as more complicated recent vehicles. When deciding what to buy, however, you need to be aware that there are restrictions on some people's driving licences that mean they can't drive the 12-seat version of the 110. The 90 station wagon seats seven, with the rear four facing inwards.

With the exception of the station wagon, the 110 has never fetched as much money second-hand as an identical 90, so if the extra metre or so of length isn't a problem they're well worth looking at. They also tow much better and carry a bigger load both by volume and weight. They'll all legally tow up to 3.5 tons on a braked trailer but the

heavier models with smaller engines tend to make slow progress. The V8, as might be expected, is well up to the task of towing.

An inspection needs to target the chassis and bulkhead for corrosion assessment before bothering with anything else. Water ingress, mainly through the roof, was a factory-fit option, and the station wagons in particular are usually damp inside from the trim absorbing it. Being commercial vehicles most have led a hard life, though with proper maintenance they're capable of decades of slavish devotion! Prices are now stable if condition is maintained, as they reflect the vehicle's future life potential rather than its age.

The Defender (1989 on)

The Defender resulted from the upgrading and renaming of the 90/110 when 'Land Rover' ceased to be used as a model name and became the manufacturer's name instead. Bearing in mind its military sales it's an apt title. The re-branding also heralded the introduction of a decent diesel engine worthy of a Land Rover product. This was the 200TDI from the recently launched Discovery. Though this rendered all Defenders superb it was the bigger, heavier versions that benefited the most, as the new diesel could cruise at well over the legal maximum speed of 70mph whereas older ones might just about qualify for a ticket if a downhill slope was steep enough and long enough. The TDI is also economical, returning 28–33mpg depending on model and use.

The Defender 90 became a super vehicle either for work or for private use. The normally aspirated diesel was still an option and continued to be used on military contracts, and 2.5- and 3.5-litre petrol-engined models also continued to be available at first, though their sales dropped when everyone realised how good the diesel was. The 200TDI was subsequently upgraded to the 300TDI.

In 1998 the 300TDI was replaced in turn by the five-cylinder 2.5-litre TD5 engine, which is still currently in use though due for replacement in 2006. This is a modern unit and provides very good performance and economy, no doubt helped by its electronics. However, there are several problems with it, including clutch and flywheel and problems with the manual gearbox. The oil pump can fall off and wreck the engine, and the cylinder heads suffer from water leakage from the head gasket and can become porous inside, allowing diesel to leak into the engine oil. This can eventually lead to the engine running on its own on the fumes. Replacement heads are expensive so look for contamination and high oil levels, low water levels, loss of the special coolant, and any noise from the clutch area.

The V8 ceased to be available soon after its ultimate utilisation in the 4-litre automatic Defender 90 limited edition. These were the only automatic Defenders produced for the UK market, though the US had had a few in their unique specification models.

Body-wise, Defender shape and configurations were unchanged from the earlier 90/110, with Pick Ups, vans, full soft tops, a high capacity 110 Pick Up, ten- and twelve-seat station wagons, and the six- or seven-seat 90. In more recent years there have been 110 crew-cabbed Pick Up Defenders, and throughout there have been 127in wheelbase models with various body configurations, though they were called 130s for marketing purposes. 110, incidentally, is the model's true wheelbase figure in inches, but the 90 is actually almost 93in.

The Meccano-like nature of the Defender means that many aren't in the same form as that in which they left the factory. Demand for second-hand 90 station wagons has always exceeded the number sold as new vehicles. Many of those on offer are actually vans that have had the seats, windows, and trim fitted later in life. No problem if done properly and reflected in the price. In most

ABOVE The V8 is the best performing engine in a Defender, but also the least economical on fuel

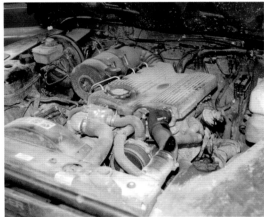

LEFT The 300 TDI is a good all-rounder both in performance and economy

LEFT The Hi Cap(acity) Defender 110 is a true working vehicle

bearing problem (see above). The R380 used on later V8s and all the other engines has problems with mainshaft wear and can be stiff trying to find gears when cold, especially second. There are clutch problems, with disc failure and arm failure, though future problems like these won't be apparent when you're buying one.

The 200TDI is fine and other than routine camshaft belt replacement is just a bit prone to head gasket and cracking problems. The later 300TDI is prone to premature cam belt failure, though there are several repair schemes to eliminate the problem and by this time in their lives most engines have probably been sorted out. The heads are prone to internal cracking but otherwise they're reliable engines.

ABOVE The Defender does not have galvanised fittings on the body so they rust like this

BELOW The Discovery is visually identical in V8 Petrol and 200TDI diesel form

cases it's possible to tell from the VIN what it was built as when new.

The construction method and use of Defenders means that corrosion of the chassis and bulkhead is the main problem and calls for careful examination. The doors all rust as well, as does the body framing on the five-door station wagon. The V8 is a reliable engine, though it can have split block and head gasket problems. In addition earlier V8-engined Defenders were fitted with the same Santana-manufactured five-speed gearbox as the 90/110 and can have the same layshaft

Discovery 1 (1989–98)

The Discovery represents good value for money and can provide you with a highly usable vehicle for a few thousand pounds. It's good mechanically, sharing the 200 and 300TDI engine with the Defender and the V8 with many other models. Another petrol-powered model used the 2-litre M16 four-cylinder engine more commonly found in the Rover 800 car.

FAR LEFT Serious corrosion of the inner steel structure is almost standard on older Discoveries

LEFT Lifting the rear floor mat will often reveal a horrible corroded mess like this, even on externally presentable Discoveries

The Discovery is very versatile and appeals to all sorts of people, which is a disadvantage when buying one as it will almost certainly have been worked hard. The majority of the bodywork is aluminium alloy over a steel shell and when in direct contact with one another these two metals are prone to corrode. The trouble is that the outer bit usually suffers less than the inner structure, so vehicles that look reasonably tidy on the outside can have serious structural flaws. Whilst I wouldn't usually suggest checking a vehicle out of logical order, on a Series I Discovery I'd always recommend checking for corrosion first as it's the most likely reason for walking away.

Target the known problem areas, which are the inner wings, especially the joint where they fix on to the bulkhead; the sill section, which is the box member that runs from the bottom of the front door pillar or 'A' post backwards under the door opening and on under the 'BC' post (this is more prone to rust on the bottom and outside and top than the inner edge, which is made of thicker steel); the rear wheelarch, which rusts where it's visible with the door open on a four-door and where the seatbelt affixes on all models; the plate that joins the wheelarch to the sill; the plate that holds the mud flap (this is inexpensive and only bolted on, so it's a good bargaining chip but not a great worry); the rear body crossmember, especially the two mounts that carry the mounting on to the chassis; and the rear floor.

The rear floor is really prone to rusting and needs the crosshead screws removing from the rearmost plastic trim in order for the carpet to be lifted. Most genuine owners won't have a problem with you doing this, but ask them first in case they object. With the carpet lifted you'll usually see a rusty mess caused by the floor coverings soaking

up water but not readily drying out again. The sponge holds water against the steel and it eventually corrodes away. It's replaceable, but costs about £100 and a couple of days' labour to do properly. Whilst a limited inspection is possible from underneath the fuel tank hides most of the problem, so it really needs the carpet to be lifted for it to be inspected properly.

If you're satisfied with the overall structural condition the next thing to check is the gearbox. From then on follow the normal examination routine, but watch for the timing belt issues and a poor gearchange on the R380 gearbox used in the 300 series. If you find sound structure and a good gearbox in the same vehicle then buy it, as it's quite a rare find.

Discovery 2 (1998–2004)

The second generation of the Discovery was hampered by having to retain the 100in wheelbase of the original, and though the back is longer, room for backseat passengers is still restricted. The rearmost seats are much better, though, as they're forward-facing and have full three-point seatbelts. They're suitable for adults but ideal for children.

Land Rover made a much better job of manufacturing the Discovery 2 and managed to reduce the corrosion by greater use of steel and by avoiding dissimilar-metal joints. The bonnet, for example, is all-aluminium whereas the rear wing is steel. Though they seem to have carried out the corrosion protection properly as well, there are nevertheless sometimes signs of the rear wings

need computer fault downloading and clearing via an OBD II socket in the car. So check all the warning lights work and aren't lit up and that there isn't a 'handbook' warning sign on the climate control if fitted. The V8 engine suffers from split block problems but this isn't detectable beforehand. This is unlikely to be a problem with a vehicle from a dealer but may well be in one at an auction. The TD5 is usually reliable but does have a few problems, though it doesn't have a timing belt to worry about.

Some Discovery 2s have air suspension at the rear and the rubber airbags are prone to leaks which can result in them sitting down at the back when not running or a total failure to rise at all. They have lots of fiddly plastic devices as well, such as the sunroof blinds and the cup holders, and many will have succumbed to little fingers forcing them in directions they were not designed to go in. However, they don't seem to have major problem areas such as corrosion to home in on, so just conduct your usual thorough check in the appropriate sequence.

ABOVE AND BELOW
The Series II Discovery is made well and is the main stock held by independents. Although rarely pushed to its limits, it will deliver if called upon

corroding because of mud traps around the door-shut area on the rear doors. Elsewhere they seem to be holding up well.

In their wisdom, though, the designers fitted more computing power than it took to land man on the Moon and it's the systems controlled by the various computers that cause most of the problems. They're not DIY friendly either, as they

Range Rover Classic (1970–95)

The Range Rover Classic was the benchmark of luxury 4x4 vehicles and through most of its production life it was the vehicle that most manufacturers tried, but failed, to emulate. To many the superb V8 petrol engine is the best bit of a Range Rover, though not everyone liked the fuel costs. A properly fitted LPG conversion is a great way to run one inexpensively but many were ruined by inappropriate diesel engine conversions. Though there are some good ones, such as the retrofit 200 and 300TDI factory kits and a few other types, in general it's wiser to stay clear of diesel conversions for several good reasons, including spare parts availability. Reliability is another issue, as they weren't all fitted very well, and another good reason is the fact that they're difficult to get insurance cover for. If you're contemplating such a vehicle there were more than 80 types of engines fitted as conversions, so you need specialist advice from one of the smaller Land Rover repair businesses on the suitability of the type of engine and on the specific vehicle in question.

The early 1970s two-door models are now

LEFT The original Range Rover became a classic in its own lifetime with an enthusiastic following

BELOW The early 2-door Range Rover is now a fast appreciating asset

RIGHT The limited edition CSK is a design icon and is arguably the classic Range Rover at its best

BELOW RIGHT Early vehicles were more off-road orientated; later ones adopted an on-road bias

BELOW The later soft dashboard versions from the 1995 model year are the most user friendly Range Rover Classics

highly collectable but do suffer from rust, rusty rear tailgates being a feature of many seen on the road. Measures subsequently taken to address some of the problems were successful and vehicles dating to the mid-1980s are quite good from that point of view and have a good specification. They've also bottomed the depreciation curve and you can buy a vehicle costing as much as £40,000 when new for as little as a couple of thousand. They're unlikely to depreciate any more if condition is maintained and will indeed appreciate in the long term.

The 1980s saw the introduction of automatic

gearboxes and factory-fit diesel engines, the 2.4 and later the 2.5 VM. They were just about OK in their day but can now go expensively wrong, so avoid them as well. A decent factory diesel engine in the form of the 200TDI eventually began to be fitted in the early 1990s and it even had an auto option. Vehicles produced for the last couple of years substituted the 300TDI. Various other ideas tried out during the last few years of production included a slightly longer wheelbase and full air suspension.

By the early 1990s it was realised that the Range Rover would need a bit of a revamp before

the new model became available, so in 1994 the interior had a makeover that included airbags within a new dash assembly. These 'soft dash' Range Rover Classics represent the model in its best form with the best interiors, the best engines – both petrol and diesel – and the most comprehensive body-protection.

The earliest two-door vehicles are now highly sought after and are regarded as classic vehicles. The first three years' production (up to the end of 1972) now enjoy exemption from road tax and several later vehicles have been rebuilt on to older chassis to claim the classic status, though in reality many of these 'rebuilds' involve nothing more than swapping the plates and altering the chassis number. If you're offered such a vehicle tread very carefully, as it may even be a stolen vehicle and as a 'ringer' you'd never actually acquire good title to it.

On all models check for corrosion in the lower body frame, including the front inner wings, sills and footwells, rear wheelarches, and rear body frame. The chassis doesn't rust so easily but it does corrode, usually starting at the rear next to where the fuel tank is mounted. Though there are quite a lot of replacement sections available and they aren't expensive they are time-consuming to fit, so it's best to avoid a vehicle that needs loads of welding unless you have the skill or the money to have it done. As with most projects, they consume more money than they'll realise if sold straight away but are worth considering if you intend to keep and use them, as they'll rise in value and repay you by having the use of them in the meanwhile.

Range Rover P38A (1994–2002)

The second generation of Range Rover had a tough job to replace the original. It was therefore thought that a very high specification vehicle would be the answer and would justify the significant asking price. Whilst the tremendously complicated computer systems that adjusted the suspension, engine, gearbox, and interior environment, and looked after all the vehicle's other electrical functions, were its strength from a sales point of view they're this model's weakness as they age.

The first thing to check is that all the electronics work OK. Don't be fooled into thinking that a fault such as the indicators not working on one side is insignificant, as it may cost £1,000 to fix this

LEFT Corrosion, in this case the front inner wing, is a well known Range Rover problem

LEFT The P38A Range Rover was a bigger and better-appointed vehicle

BELOW But a lot of the refinement was electronic-based and notoriously unreliable. When they're good they're great, but when they mess around they are horrid

RIGHT Corrosion is not a big issue on these Range Rovers, but the lower tailgate is one area to check

BELOW The V8 is a great engine, though suffers internal cracking, while the diesel is sluggish and noisy, especially in automatic form

ABOVE The third version of the Range Rover is a superb and reliable vehicle, much better than its predecessor

seemingly trivial problem. Another favourite is for the stepper motors in the heating system to fail and for cold air to be blown into one of the footwells all the time. A proper repair is a few hundred pounds and it's not unknown to see a polythene seat cover stuffed into the air duct as a cheaper solution to the problem. The windows also play up and sometimes individual doors refuse to open.

The only corrosion area seems to be the bottom of the rear lower tailgate. The 2000 model year vehicles had quite a few revisions and are much more reliable, so look for all the warning lights coming on and going off as they ought to check all the other functions, including the air suspension. If it's a V8 check the waterworks and if these are all working properly look at the rest of the vehicle.

Range Rover L322 (2002 on)

Seemingly a much better vehicle than its predecessor, the third generation Range Rover has not only tremendous electronic power but also, seemingly, a higher level of reliability. There are no specific points to target prior to a full inspection so just work your way through the standard checkout.

Freelander (1997–2006)

The Freelander was Land Rover's first foray into the 'small 4x4' market and they produced a really capable vehicle that was a first for them in that it didn't have a separate chassis and had full independent suspension.

In an effort to create a tough vehicle the shell is very strong and they've done a super protection job so that corrosion appears not to be an issue, even on the oldest vehicles. However, the engine and gearbox were borrowed from the Rover car range and the 'K' Series petrol engine suffers a few water-related problems.

The diesels seem to be fine. The main areas of weakness are the transmission to the rear, as the independent rear-drive unit on the gearbox can fail prematurely, as can the central viscous coupling, its support bearings, and the rear differential itself. So after the engine and before anything else, check for signs of noise and

RIGHT
The Freelander was the first Land Rover to have independent suspension and no separate chassis. Available in 3- or 5-door estate forms, the latter is the most popular and hence more valuable

FAR RIGHT This is the Freelander's viscous coupling and the carrier bearings for it are often noisy, although easy to replace

BELOW The drive to the Freelander's rear end is problematic

harshness in the transmission, and for tyre scrabbling noises that would suggest the viscous coupling is faulty.

In some sales environments such as auctions it's not unknown for a troublesome driveline to be totally removed and the vehicle to be operating in front drive only, so be warned! The electronics seem to be reliable and many faults such as the hill descent not working are a result of wiring problems (in this case being broken at the bottom of the gearlever).

General problems

There are some items fitted to Land Rovers that are worthy of special attention as they're often problematical and are fitted to many different vehicles in the line up.

V8 engine problems

The V8 Rover engine is a well-proven design but in its later years it became less reliable. The early ones suffer from wear in the valve gear, making the top end noisy, and they're also prone to oil leaks. The EFI system isn't as reliable as modern engines, as it uses older technology. All engines suffer a bit from cylinder head gasket problems but the later ones, especially in 3.9/4.0-litre and 4.6-litre form, suffer from the bore splitting behind the liner and letting water into the sump. A new block is the cure, but at over £2,500 in bits alone. Specialist machining and a new liner might be no more than a semi-permanent solution, as the other cylinders might crack as well. Check very carefully for white oil, as it gets emulsified, and for water consumption on a test run.

'K' Series engine problems

The petrol engines in Freelanders have developed a bit of a reputation for problems associated with the cylinder head and its gasket. Both the 1.8-litre four-cylinder and the 2.5-litre V6 are from a family of engines also used in other vehicles, such as the Rover 200 and 25, the MGF, and the Rover 75. They're collectively known as the 'K' Series and they're available in all sorts of configurations from 1.1 litres to 2.5. They also have a bit of a reputation for troubles in the waterworks department.

The 'K' Series engine was an innovative design. It has liners surrounded by water set in the block, held down by the cylinder head with ten long bolts passing through the head right down to the main bearing area. This allowed the opposing mechanical forces within the structure of the engine to cancel each other out to a large degree, meaning the engine was light in weight and small in dimension. This is actually a really sweet, willing engine in all forms, but the area on the top of the liners where the gasket seals against the cylinder head isn't large and the gasket material is prone to let water into the cylinders. The result is usually a catastrophic failure, especially if the driver never looks at the temperature reading and runs it until it stops. However, there are initial symptoms such as water use, steam from the exhaust, a sort of burnt smell in the filler tank, and brown discoloured

water. The water might need topping up every few days but will eventually need fixing properly.

The cure, as long as no other damage has been caused, is to fit the later type of revised gasket and a new set of the long bolts that hold the head down. It's about £100 for the bits and about a day's work, depending on how speedy you are. Having the head refaced isn't

ABOVE The Rover V8 suffers head gasket failure, though later engines are better in this respect

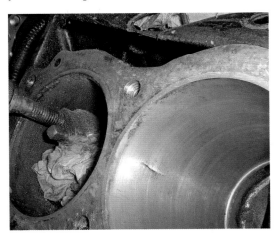

LEFT They all suffer cracks in the block behind the liners, and especially prone are the later engines in the P38A Range Rover

BELOW The Rover K series in the Freelander is prone to head gasket failure

recommended unless it's damaged or warped, a thorough clean and a check with a straight edge being sufficient on most. Since the tension has to be taken off it you should always fit a new timing belt at the same time – if they're not replaced they don't last as long as they ought to.

This failure of the silicone ring in the gasket around the cylinders has led to many engines being replaced under warranty by Land Rover. They didn't make the engine themselves but bought it in from Rover. However, the collapse of the MG Rover Company means that supplies have now dried up and repair is the only option. The usual problems, if the gasket failure isn't noticed in time, result from the dry engine overheating so that the pistons start to melt and pick up on the bore surface. Sometimes the bottom end gives problems too if the oil gets too much water in it and stops lubricating properly so that the big ends fail. If there's been a problem with a piston picking up it's possible to replace liners and pistons as needed. There are also a few second-hand engines available from accident-damaged cars such as the 418 Rover and the 1.8 petrol-powered Rover 75. It's possible to fit the 2-litre four-cylinder version too. The 1.1 and 1.4 also fit, though performance will suffer. In all cases the appropriate ECU for the engine ought to be fitted but in practice the 2.0 will run on the 1.8 ECU without problem.

The V6 2.5 litre is just as prone to trouble and is more work to fix as two heads need to be removed and space is a bit limited in the Freelander engine bay.

Freelanders with engines manufactured from 2000 onwards are supposed to be better than the early cars but they're still prone to problems, so those fitted with engines under warranty ought to have the revised type of head gasket already. The revision is much better but not a cure-all. It's really just a shift of emphasis, so now they'll only probably have head problems at some point as opposed to definitely having them.

If you're thinking of buying one don't let these problems put you off such a super vehicle. The diesel TD4 is a good engine but the four-cylinder petrol one is even better as it drives well, is just as economical, and costs a lot less to buy. The V6 is even better to drive but isn't so economical, though those used to V8 Land Rovers will think it is.

You need to take the vehicle for a long run after checking the water level so that you can check for signs of overheating. You also need to watch for burnt smells or discoloration, usually brown, in the header tank.

It may sound a bit of a weird plan but I'd try to buy one *with* engine problems, as the price will be significantly depressed by a factor of hundreds if

RIGHT The Freelander is a great Land Rover, spoilt only by the petrol engine's lack of reliability

not thousands of pounds. You can then spend the saving rebuilding the engine with the up-to-date revised gasket and new bolts, etc. You then know that the engine ought to be fine for quite a long time and will still have saved some money. As a workshop job it's usually about £500 to sort out including new oil, timing belt, and so on. Some garages charge more than others for labour but the maximum ought to be less than £1,000, even if the cylinder head needs to be skimmed.

Land Rover 2.5 and Turbo Diesel engine problems

The Land Rover Turbo Diesel engine seemed like a good idea at the time but it has suffered tremendous problems in service. It wasn't sufficiently developed and the company tried to get away with a simple turbo addition to improve performance without enough upgrades to the 2.5 normally aspirated engine, which is quite reliable. It was only fitted to 90/110 Land Rovers from October 1986 to October 1990, when it was superseded by the 200TDI diesel engine.

The Turbo engine has quite a lot of problems associated with running hot, including cylinder head failure, piston failure, blocks cracking in the bores, valve seats falling out, and oil pump problems, as well as the timing belt breaking or

slipping due to oil contamination. It's worse in the 110 and 127 Land Rovers, as they run at heavier weights. I'd suggest you try to avoid buying a vehicle with this engine as its power unit. If you can't resist one remember that the 90 is the most reliable, being lighter in weight.

The non-Turbo version, often called the 2.5 normally aspirated, isn't as powerful but is more reliable, so either buy one with this engine or the later TDI. In fact many vehicles originally fitted with this engine have been retrofitted with the TDI

ABOVE This is the sort of damage that happens when the valve seats fall out of the 2.5 Turbo diesel, although the engine was repairable

LEFT Turbo unit, highlighted in blue on a specially prepared 90 exhibition chassis, is responsible for many engine failures as it overstretched the original design

when they were quite young. It's also revealing
that the UK military went straight from the non-
Turbo engine to the TDI, avoiding the turbo 2.5
altogether.

VM engine problems

When Land Rover were looking to use diesel
power in the Range Rover they spent lots of
money developing the V8 engine for diesel use in
conjunction with Perkins engines in
Peterborough. However, it never worked properly
and time was short so they decided to fit a
bought-in unit instead and settled on the Italian
VM 2.4 engine that had been used in the SD1
Rover car. It was a turbocharged unit and ran
well in the Range Rover, though it was noisy and
less refined than the V8. Called the Turbo D, it
went on sale in 1986 and in 1989 was uprated to
2.5 litres. However, it suffered from cylinder head
and gasket problems and piston and liner problems
and was very expensive to repair, so in November
1992 it was replaced by the TDI engine as used in
the Discovery.

   Though the Turbo D was a good engine when
working, the expense of repair and the difficulty of
getting bits means that they're best avoided. They
were quite rare on the UK market anyway and
found better favour in export markets, especially
Italy where the engines were made. Many surviving
UK vehicles have been fitted with other engines –
such as the TDI – to keep them running.

200TDI and 300TDI engine problems

The TDI engines are by far the best diesels to be
built at Solihull and are generally very reliable, but
they're a bit prone to head gasket failures and
cracking and the front pulley can come loose,
especially if dirty when reassembled following a
timing belt change. The 200TDI has timing belt
problems resulting in premature wear, and the
tension mechanism can give problems too. This
was supposed to be rectified on the 300TDI but
these have even more belt problems, including
manufacturing defects. There are various timing
belt modification schemes applicable to various
groups of engine numbers.

   They also suffer head cracking, but as with
most of the engine problems this won't be
apparent on a road test if the engine isn't
overheating and will only appear (if ever) as a
breakdown. It's not all bad news, though, as in
general they're very reliable units and most of the
problems will have been sorted out by now. These
power units have been used in the Discovery 1,
the Range Rover Classic, and the Defender.

TD5 engine problems

Fitted to the Discovery 2 and the Defender from
1987, this is a superb engine to drive but
because of its electronic complexity it isn't DIY-
friendly. It has other issues as well, such as the oil
pump coming loose, the complicated flywheel
assembly on manual gearboxes giving trouble,
problems with water use resulting from cylinder
head gasket failure, and diesel oil leaking into the
lubricating oil from porosity in the cylinder head
fuel gallery. It doesn't have a timing belt as a chain
drive is used, which works perfectly. The fly by
wire throttle system is linked directly to the engine
computer and any faults need the services of a
diagnostic system linked to the OBD II socket.
Though it sounds complicated it's normal on most
vehicles now. Though the engine has problems
there are many that are running fine, so I wouldn't
avoid buying a vehicle just because it was fitted
with this engine.

LT77 gearbox problems

The LT77 (Land Rover Transmission with 77mm
centres between shafts) has a few problems, being
especially renowned for premature wear on the
mainshaft where it enters the transfer box. This can
often be detected, before it fails totally and drive is
lost, by being a bit rough with the clutch when
changing direction, ie reverse after going forward or
first after reverse. There's often a deep, very

metallic clunk as the wear takes up. This should not be confused with the normal play or 'shunt' that's normal in the transmission of vehicles like this, especially as they get more miles on them.

This gearbox was originally designed for the SD1 Rover car but was beefed up for other applications, including the 4x4 Land Rover. It wears in use and causes selection problems but will carry on for some time like this, especially if the operator learns to be gentle with it. The fifth speed is a real bonus on motorways.

As it was fitted to most 90/110s and Defenders, Range Rovers from 1983, and Discoveries, it's difficult not to own one if you buy a Land Rover. It's not really a problem, though, as it does actually give quite good service. As any synchromesh issues will diminish when hot you need to drive them from cold when testing a vehicle.

R380 gearbox problems

The R380 is an upgrade of the LT77 main gearbox and is identifiable by its reverse gear being opposite fifth rather than next to first. This was done in an effort to improve the gear change. The problems with the tailshaft still happen but a revised gear means that the R380 is far less prone to it than the older LT77. Fitted to Defenders, Discovery 1 and 2, Range Rover Classic and the P38 from 1994, it's quite reliable, but does suffer from selection problems as it ages, especially second gear. This is most noticeable when it's cold, and some won't engage until the box has warmed up. It's advisable to test-drive one from cold so that you know if it has any problems, since these can disappear once it's at operating temperature.

Power steering problems

Though a worthwhile addition to coil-sprung Land Rovers the power steering systems used on the original Range Rovers, 90/110s, Defenders, and the Discovery 1 are notorious for leaking. As the sector shaft wears along with its supporting bearings it allows sideways movement which lets hydraulic oil slip past the main seal. A worn-out box is characterised by red fluid dripping from it. Replacement isn't expensive, costing about £300 for a reconditioned item to be fitted. A new seal will sometimes cure the problem if it's just a worn seal that's causing it, but won't last for long if the bearings are worn as well. Leaks will fail an MoT test but a small amount of dampness around the seal is common and acceptable. To test the box wind full lock on in each direction with the engine running and look for traces of oil on the floor below the box, or watch the bottom of the box whilst someone else turns the steering wheel. A sheet of newspaper under the box will help show any fresh fluid leaking out.

A leak isn't a reason to dismiss an otherwise sound prospective purchase, though the replacement cost ought to be factored into the price negotiations.

Chassis repairs

In the UK the steel chassis of Land Rovers tends to corrode with rust. This is partly due to the operating environment, with water, road salt, and farmyard chemicals all assisting the corrosion process. In addition cost-saving measures in the early 1970s meant that from about 1973 cheaper quality steel was used that's more prone to corrosion. The aluminium alloy used in the bodies was also changed and that too became more prone to corrosion.

Things didn't improve with time and it's only more recent vehicles such as the Discovery 2 and Freelander that have properly addressed the problem, probably with the help of engineers from BMW when they owned the company. So if you buy a Land Rover made between 1973 and 1997 it will invariably be corroded to some extent, with certain models – such as the Discovery – being especially bad.

You'll probably be buying a vehicle that's had some form of repair to the chassis and/or bodywork. In the UK the annual MoT test is failed if corrosion exists in a structural member or within 30cm of one, and most of a Land Rover's chassis and lower floor is structural because of its proximity to seat mounts, body mounts, and so on. Repairs are acceptable if they reinstate the same integral strength as the original, which essentially means steel of a similar strength and thickness welded to sound original material. So a chassis is fine with a 2mm steel patch seam-welded to it or a replacement crossmember seam welded on. A thin patch tack-welded on and covered with black goo or a fibreglass repair aren't acceptable.

Likewise, properly welded steel patches or a full replacement floor welded in are acceptable repairs for a Discovery floor, whereas an aluminium, pop-riveted patch isn't if it's within 300mm of the seatbelt or any other mounting point. An aluminium patch is acceptable on a Defender rear floor as it's of aluminium manufacture and doesn't carry the seat or seatbelt loadings. As a guide, proper repairs have a clear metallic ring if you tap them with a small hammer or spanner. Poor repairs and corrosion give a dull thud.

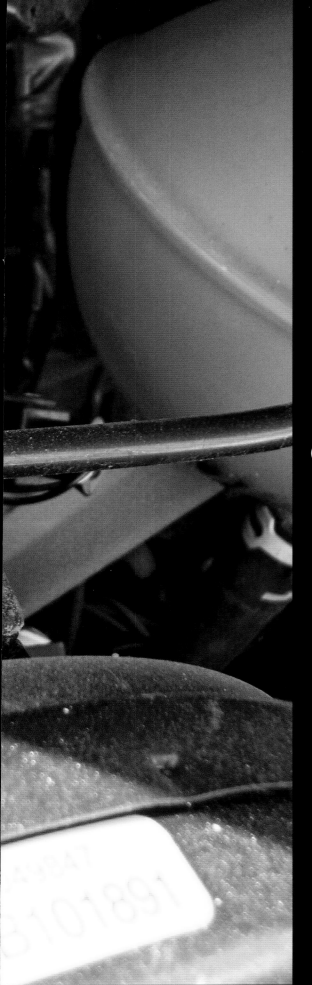

Decoding Land Rover chassis numbers

The Land Rover chassis or VIN number has two separate functions. One is as a unique identifier used to confirm that the actual vehicle, the paperwork held by the owner, and the record on the DVLA computer all correspond. The second is to determine what the vehicle actually is – where it was made and what configuration it took when it was manufactured.

Before the adoption of the VIN system Land Rovers were identified by numbers stamped into the metal of the chassis. Like VIN numbers these were unique to each vehicle and were recorded against the registration in the card index systems operated by the registration authorities and in the vehicle's logbook. With the introduction of the nationwide computer system based in Swansea in the early 1970s this information was transferred to the computer-generated V5 registration document. The chassis number also identifies what the vehicle was built as, and in some cases the year in which it was manufactured.

The chassis numbers for almost all Land Rovers built from 1948 to 1979 consisted of two groups of numbers within a sequence of about eight numbers, followed in some cases by a letter. The first three numbers signified the actual model, the steering position, and the market destination, and these were followed by a serial number. The serial numbers started at '1' for each type of vehicle. So, for example. '35500452' identifies a vehicle as a Range Rover right-hand-drive home market model (355), and it's the 452nd of that type to be built.

In February 1975 the system changed slightly: the serial numbers for every model became consecutive but still started with the three-digit prefix defining the vehicle type and specification. So '35652499F' is a Range Rover right-hand-drive export model (356) and its serial number is 52499. The 'F' suffix indicates there's been a major change of mechanical specification and is there to make ordering spare parts easier – in this example the change from suffix 'E' occurred when, amongst other things, the exhaust system changed to a twin tailpipe arrangement.

In the 1970s Land Rovers followed a similar numbering system to Range Rovers, but prior to that even more information could be found hidden in the chassis numbers. The first ones, from 1948, included a model year identifier. This model year went from autumn to autumn, so the 1951 model year, for example, went from September 1950 to August 1951.

There were five distinct numbering systems used during Series I production and there isn't the room to go into full details here, but after that things settled down and the same system was subsequently used right through Series II and for Series III up to 1979. The year identifier, however, was dropped following the introduction of the Series IIA in August 1961.

An example of an earlier number would be '111801110', the '111' indicating it as an 88in wheelbase petrol home market Series I, the '8' being for the 1958 model year, and the serial number identifying it as the 1,110th built. An example of a later number would be '34500028A', which tells us that it's a 109in six-cylinder right-hand-drive home market Series IIA and that it's the 28th made. It dates from 1967, but this can't be ascertained from the chassis number. Another example is '91600636A', being a 109in Diesel Series III right-hand-drive home market vehicle. It was manufactured in 1972, but again that's not found in the chassis number.

The way of numbering chassis changed in October 1979 following the adoption of an alphanumerical system of 14 digits, later increased to 17. This is referred to as the VIN

(Vehicle Identification Number). Its introduction brought a Europe-wide standard system into play where some of the alphanumerical sequence was unique to an individual manufacturer, while some – such as the code for the country of manufacture and its position in the VIN – was common to them all, as was the number of digits used. In a 17-digit VIN the first 11 (originally nine) indicate the vehicle's details and the last six are the serial number, in the case of Land Rover a sequence applied to all vehicle production starting at 100001 in October 1979.

Below is a list of some of the most common letters found. This list is by no means exhaustive, as a full listing of all chassis and VIN combinations would fill more than this book several times over, but it includes those that might be most useful and apply to post-1979 vehicles. Pre-1979 details and those up to the mid-1980s can be researched at BMIHT (see Appendix 1 for contact details).

The US, Canadian, and some other export markets employ a broadly similar system which is used on Land Rover products destined for these territories, but whilst some of the 17 digits will correspond with the UK models others won't. There's also a random check digit applicable to an individual vehicle, so it's best to confirm the build details of a specific vehicle with the manufacturer if necessary. Though the vehicles may look the same they're usually manufactured to a different specification for the different markets. Many second-hand Land Rovers are being imported back into this country, especially from Japan. It's therefore useful to be able to identify this type of vehicle when ordering spare parts or carrying out work on them.

BELOW Vehicles built over the last few years have a VIN behind the windscreen as it is clearly visible for checking purposes by prospective purchasers or MoT testers. It is also tamper resistant as it needs the screen out to get to it as on this Freelander

VIN decoder

LETTERS 1-2-3

SA	Rover (not used initially)
L	Land Rover (SAL is now Land Rover)

LETTERS 4-5

LA	Discovery 3/LR3
LB	Series III
LD	90/110/130
LH	Range Rover (Classic)
LJ	Discovery
LM	Range Rover (L322)
LN	Freelander
LP	Range Rover (P38A)
LS	Range Rover Sport

LETTER 6 (WHEELBASE)

A	88in Series III
A	Range Rover
A	Freelander
A	90in Defender XD
A	Discovery 2 (Japan)
A	Sport standard trim
A	Range Rover standard trim (L322)
B	88in 1/2-ton Military
B	108in Range Rover
B	110in Heavy Duty
B	Commercial Freelander
C	109in Series III
C	130in Defender XD
C	108in Range Rover
D	109in Series III 1-ton Military
D	Honda Crossroads (Discovery)
E	100in Range Rover (CAL)
F	108in Range Rover (CAL)
F	Freelander Sport
G	100in
H	110in Defender (STD)
J	110in 1-tonne
J	Honda Discovery (Japan)
J	Discovery 3 (Japan)
J	Sport (Japan)
K	130in Defender (STD)
M	Special Vehicle
N	109in 1-ton 12v
N	Discovery (California spec)
P	109in 1-ton 24v
R	110in Defender (Military)
R	Discovery PI (Japan)
S	110in Defender V8 (Military)
V	90in Defender (STD)
V	Range Rover (3.5 NAS)
X	Range Rover Special
X	90in Military 24v
X	90in Defender (California)
X	90in Defender (Turkey)

LETTER 7 (BODY STYLE)

A	Truck Cab
A	Hard Top
A	Pick Up/Hood
A	Two-door Range Rover
A	Three-door Discovery
A	Three-door Freelander
A	Four-door Discovery 3/Sport
B	Three-door Series III Station Wagon
B	Three-door Station Wagon (90, 110, Range Rover)
B	Three-door Discovery
B	Five-door Freelander
C	Lightweight (MSA)
C	Defender L/W (Spain)
D	Defender Military (Spain)
E	Two-door Crew Cab
F	Four-door Crew Cab non-HCPU
H	110in or 130in HCPU
M	Five-door Series III 109in Station Wagon
M	Four-door Range Rover and Discovery
M	Four-door 110in and Defender Station Wagon
M	Four-door Range Rover L322
R	Four-door Monteverdi Conversion
1	Four-door Station Wagon (NAS)
3	Three-door Station Wagon (NAS)

LETTER 8 (ENGINE TYPE)

A	4.0 V8 petrol injection (EFI) low compression non-catalytic converter
A	1.8 4cyl K16 Freelander
A	2.5 4cyl diesel naturally aspirated
A	4.4 V8 petrol injection
B	2.5 4cyl turbo diesel (Falcon)
B	4.0 V8 petrol injection (EFI) low compression non-catalytic converter
B	2.0 4cyl turbo diesel Freelander
C	2.5 4cyl diesel naturally aspirated
C	4.6 V8 petrol injection (EFI) low compression non-catalytic converter
C	1.8 4cyl petrol (K16) Freelander
C	3.0 V6 diesel TD6
D	2.5 4cyl petrol carb
D	4.6 V8 petrol injection low compression non-catalytic converter
D	1.8 4cyl petrol (K16) Freelander
E	2.4 4cyl (VM) diesel Range Rover Classic
E	2.5 4cyl turbo diesel non-exhaust gas recirculating and non-catalytic converter
E	2.0 4cyl (TD4 BMW) diesel Freelander
F	2.5 4cyl turbo diesel (TDI) (Gemini) non-catalytic converter
F	1.8 4cyl petrol (K16) Freelander

G	2.25 4cyl diesel Series III
G	2.5 V6 petrol (KV6) Freelander leaded fuel
H	2.25 4cyl petrol Series III
H	2.5 V6 petrol (KV6) Freelander air-conditioning non-catalytic converter
J	4.6 V8 petrol injection (EFI) high compression catalytic converter
J	2.5 V6 (KV6) ethanol fuel compatible Freelander
K	2.5 V6 petrol (KV6) leaded fuel Freelander
K	2.5 4cyl turbo diesel (TDI) exhaust gas recirculating and/or catalytic converter
K	2.5 4cyl turbo diesel (TDI) cooled exhaust gas recirculating and/or catalytic converter
K	4.4 6cyl diesel Santana
L	3.5 V8 petrol injection (EFI) Range Rover
L	3.5 V8 petrol injection (EFI) Discovery
M	3.9 V8 petrol injection (EFI) Range Rover
M	3.9 V8 petrol injection (EFI) Defender
M	4.0 V8 petrol injection (EFI) high compression catalytic converter
N	2.5 4cyl turbo diesel (VM) Range Rover
P	2.6 Straight 6cyl petrol Series III
P	4.0 V8 petrol injection high compression catalytic converter North American specification
R	4.6 V8 petrol injection high compression catalytic converter automatic transmission North American specification
S	3.4 6cyl diesel Santana
T	3.4 6cyl petrol Santana
V	2.0 4cyl leaded petrol
V	3.5 V8 petrol injection non-catalytic converter
W	2.5 6cyl turbo diesel (BMW) Range Rover
X	3.9 4cyl diesel (Perkins)
Y	2.0 4cyl unleaded petrol
Y	2.0 petrol injection (T16) Discovery/Defender
Z	3.9 4cyl diesel (Isuzu)
1	3.5 V8 petrol injection (EFI) North American specification
1	4.0 V8 petrol injection (EFI) low compression automatic transmission Discovery 2
1	2.5 5cyl turbo diesel (TD5 EU1 specification) Defender
1	2.7 V6 turbo diesel Discovery 3 (Ford)
2	3.9 V8 petrol injection (4.0 EFI) North American specification
2	4.0 V8 petrol injection (EFI) high compression catalytic converter
2	4.0 V8 petrol injection (EFI) low compression non-catalytic converter
2	4.2 V6 turbo diesel

3	4.2 V8 petrol injection Range Rover North American specification
3	4.0 V8 petrol injection (EFI) low compression non-catalytic converter
3	4.2 V8 supercharged petrol Range Rover Sport
4	4.2 V8 supercharged petrol L322 Range Rover 3
4	4.6 V8 petrol injection (EFI) North American specification
4	4.0 V8 petrol injection high compression manual transmission Discovery 2
4	4.0 V6 petrol Discovery 3
5	4.0 V6 petrol high compression catalytic converter North America only
5	2.0 4cyl petrol (T16) non-catalytic converter Discovery 1
5	2.5 5cyl turbo diesel (TD5 EU3 specification) Defender
5	4.4 V8 petrol Discovery 3/Sport/L322 Jaguar
6	2.5 4cyl turbo diesel (TDI) exhaust gas recirculating and/or catalytic converter
6	4.6 V8 petrol high compression catalytic converter North American specification
7	2.5 5cyl turbo diesel (TD5) exhaust gas recirculating non-catalytic converter
7	2.5 5cyl turbo diesel (TD5) rest of world specification Defender
8	2.5 5cyl turbo diesel (TD5) exhaust gas recirculating and catalytic converter (Storm)
8	2.5 5cyl turbo diesel (TD5) Defender
9	2.8 6cyl petrol (BMW M52) Defender
9	2.5 5cyl turbo diesel (TD5) exhaust gas recirculating catalytic converter (Storm)

LETTER 9
(TRANSMISSION AND STEERING)

1	Right-hand-drive four-speed manual
1	Right-hand-drive five-speed automatic
2	Left-hand-drive four-speed manual
2	Left-hand-drive five-speed automatic
3	Right-hand-drive five-speed automatic
3	Right-hand-drive six-speed automatic
4	Left-hand-drive five-speed automatic
4	Left-hand-drive four-speed automatic Defender
4	Left-hand-drive six-speed automatic
5	Right-hand-drive four-speed + overdrive
6	Left-hand-drive four-speed + overdrive
7	Right-hand-drive five-speed manual
7	Right-hand-drive six-speed manual
8	Left-hand-drive five-speed manual
8	Left-hand-drive six-speed automatic
9	Right-hand-drive six-speed manual
0	Left-hand-drive six-speed manual

LETTER 10 (MODEL YEAR)

A	88/109 Series III
A	Land Rover 90 and 110
B	Land Rover 110 Facelift
B	Range Rover Phase 2 (P38A)
C	Range Rover 1986
D	Range Rover 1987
E	Model year 1988
F	Model year 1989
G	Model year 1990
H	Model year 1991
J	Model year 1992
K	Model year 1993
L	Model year 1994
M	Model year 1995
N	Model year 1996
T	Model year 1996
V	Model year 1997
W	Model year 1998
X	Model year 1999
Y	Model year 2000
1	Model year 2001
2	Model year 2002
3	Model year 2003
4	Model year 2004
5	Model year 2005
6	Model year 2006

LETTER 11 (ASSEMBLY LOCATIONS)

A	Solihull, England
C	Zimbabwe KD (knocked down)
D	Thailand
F	CKD (completely knocked down) pack, rest of world
J	Malaysia KD
K	Kenya KD
N	Morocco KD
T	Brazil KD
V	South Africa KD
W	Turkey KD
Y	Australia KD

Use list to decode the VIN of vehicles that you're thinking of purchasing. For example, a vehicle with 'SALLDVBH7AA213324' as its VIN can be identified as a Land Rover (SAL) 90, 110, or 130 (LD) with a 90in wheelbase (V), a three-door Station Wagon body (B), and a 2.25-litre petrol engine (H), and is a right-hand-drive five-speed manual (7) built before 1986 (A) at Solihull (A). So when you look at this vehicle as a prospective purchase you know it started life as a proper factory-built 90 Station Wagon, and since it now has a 2.5 diesel engine you'll know it's had an engine swap at some time. You also know that since it's an A prefix registration the date identifier of 1984 fits. Now all you have to do is check the number on the chassis hasn't been tampered with and agrees with the VIN plate and all the paperwork and it's safe to buy the vehicle, so long as the database check is OK.

Location of VIN and chassis numbers

The chassis number or VIN are usually found embossed into the metal of the chassis frame, stamped in a metal plate that's riveted or screwed to the bodywork, or on later vehicles on a plastic label affixed to the bodywork with adhesive. On vehicles manufactured since the mid-1990s it can also be found on a plate visible in the lower left-hand corner of the windscreen. Though older chassis number plates were hand stamped they were machine stamped from the early 1960s and the digits are in a straight line. In more recent years they've been embossed from behind to make forgeries easier to detect.

The VIN also has the maximum vehicle weight (or MAM, standing for maximum authorised mass), the maximum weight including a trailer, and the maximum front (1) and minimum rear (2) axle weights. If you deduct the top weight (the MAM) from the second weight down (the gross train weight) it will give the maximum trailer weight. This is usually 3,500kg on most Land Rovers but some have a lower authorised tow weight. In the bottom corner there's a box called 'Paint' and the code it gives will identify the vehicle colour. However, Land Rover aren't very good at putting the details in this box.

RIGHT As well as telling you who made this Range Rover, the VIN also gives the type approval number, the VIN number, the gross weight, maximum weight with trailer, front and rear axle maximum weights, the colour code and trim type. By using this and decoding the VIN (4.6 auto RHD) it enables you to confirm it is as built

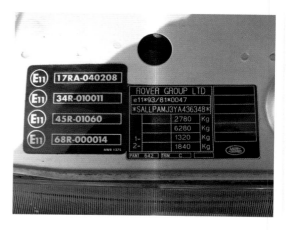

Land Rover Series I

80

The chassis number is found on the left-hand side engine mount and on the instruction plate in the cab. Very early ones had it on a plate under the bonnet.

86/107

Stamped on the rear left-hand spring shackle bracket and on the cab instruction plate.

88/109

Stamped on the front right chassis leg on the inside of earlier vehicles and the outside of later ones, on the thicker bit just above the spring pin, and on the cab instruction plate.

Series II

Stamped on the outer front right-hand chassis leg and on the instruction plate in the cab.

Series III

The chassis number is stamped on the front right chassis leg on the outside and on the instruction plate in the cab of early vehicles. Later ones had it on a plate on the front panel near to the battery, and during the last few years it was on a plate on the bulkhead.

90/110/127 and all Defenders

The VIN is stamped on the outside of the chassis on the right-hand front jacking point and on a plate riveted to the brake pedal assembly under the bonnet. Later ones also have the number in the bottom left of the windscreen.

Range Rover Classic

The number is stamped in the chassis within the square made by the steering box mounting bolts on the outside of the right-hand front chassis leg. It's also on a plate riveted to the front panel and on later ones also appears in the lower left of the windscreen.

Range Rover P38a

The VIN is stamped on the outside of the front right chassis leg, on a sticker on the front panel, and in the lower right of the windscreen.

Range Rover 3

The VIN is stamped into the body shell at the front, on a sticker on the bonnet slam panel, and is visible in the lower left of the windscreen.

Discovery 1

The VIN is stamped in the chassis within the square made by the steering box mounting bolts on the outside of the right-hand front chassis leg. It's also on a plate riveted to the front panel and on later ones appears in the lower left of the windscreen.

Discovery 2

The VIN is stamped on the outside of the front right chassis leg, on a sticker on the front panel, and in the lower right of the windscreen.

Discovery 3

The VIN is stamped in the chassis at the front, on a sticker on the front panel, and on a plate visible in the lower left of the windscreen. Note how the sticker also carries the type approval details and the colour, both as a code and as a description.

Freelander

The VIN is stamped in the steel shell at the rear of the engine bay, on a sticker stuck to the left-hand side B post (visible when you open the left front door), and appears in the lower left of the windscreen.

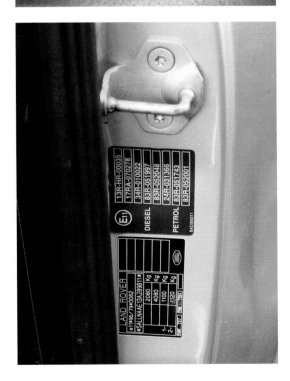

Appendices

Appendix 1

USEFUL CONTACTS

AA (vehicle check)
0800 056 6000
0800 015 8982
www.theAA.com

BMIHT Gaydon
British Motor Industry Heritage Trust
Heritage Motor Centre
Banbury Road
Gaydon
Warwickshire
CV35 0BJ
01926 641188

Brightwells 4x4 Auctioneers
Easter Court
Leominster
Herefordshire
HR6 0DE
01568 611325
vehicles@brightwells.com

Car Inspection Co
0800 146869

Citizens Advice Bureau
See your local telephone directory or
www.nacab.org.uk

DVLA website and hotline
www.dvla.gov.uk
08702400010

Equifax (personal credit check)
www.equifax.co.uk

Experian (personal credit check)
www.experian.co.uk

HPI (checks for Legal Title, Vehicle Condition Alert
Register (VCAR) for crash damage, and Police
Stolen Vehicle Database)
01722 422422

Land Rover Traceability
Traceability Dept
Land Rover Ltd
Lode Lane
Solihull
West Midlands
B92 8NW
01217222424
01217004524 (direct line)

MoT Hotline
Vehicle Operator Services Agency
0870606 0440
www.vosa.gov.uk

RAC Vehicle Inspections
0870 533 3660

Trading Standards
See your local telephone directory

Appendix 2

NEED/WANT CRIB SHEET

Want	Need	Don't need	Doesn't matter
4x2 vehicle	☐	☐	☐
4x4 vehicle	☐	☐	☐
Land Rover product	☐	☐	
New	☐	☐	
Second-hand	☐	☐	
Long warranty	☐	☐	
Extreme off-road ability	☐	☐	☐
Moderate off-road ability	☐	☐	☐
Minor off-road ability	☐	☐	
Good on-road manners	☐	☐	☐
Good towing characteristics	☐	☐	☐
High cruising speed (70mph)	☐	☐	☐
Defender	☐	☐	☐
Freelander	☐	☐	☐
Discovery	☐	☐	☐
Range Rover	☐	☐	☐
Range Rover Sport	☐	☐	
Diesel	☐		☐
Petrol	☐	☐	☐
LPG	☐	☐	☐
Good fuel economy	☐	☐	
Low toll/bridge charges	☐	☐	☐
High-specification interior	☐	☐	☐
Posh-looking exterior	☐	☐	☐
Forward-facing seats	☐	☐	☐
Cloth seat facings	☐	☐	☐
Leather seat facings	☐	☐	☐
Air conditioning	☐	☐	☐
Family-friendly	☐	☐	
Task suitability	☐	☐	☐

Want	Need	Don't need	Doesn't matter
VAT reclaimable	☐	☐	☐
Low company car tax classification	☐	☐	☐
Low Road Tax	☐	☐	☐
Nil rate Historic Tax Class	☐	☐	☐
Automatic gearbox	☐	☐	☐
Manual gearbox	☐	☐	☐
Two doors	☐	☐	☐
Three doors	☐	☐	☐
Four doors	☐	☐	☐
Five doors	☐	☐	☐
Soft Top	☐	☐	☐
Hard Top	☐	☐	☐
Two seats	☐	☐	☐
Three seats	☐	☐	☐
Five seats	☐	☐	☐
Seven seats	☐	☐	☐
Nine seats	☐	☐	☐
Ten seats	☐	☐	☐
Twelve seats	☐	☐	☐
Under 21-year-old drivers	☐	☐	☐
High internal weight carrying capacity	☐	☐	☐
High internal volume	☐	☐	☐
Tow up to 2 tons	☐	☐	☐
Tow up to 3.5 tons	☐	☐	☐
Tow up to 4 tons with supplementary braking system	☐	☐	☐
Low depreciation rate	☐	☐	☐
High residual	☐	☐	☐
Low funding costs	☐		
Main dealer buying environment	☐	☐	
Auction buying environment	☐	☐	
Independent dealer buying environment	☐	☐	
Private vendor buying environment	☐	☐	
Young/low mileage vehicle	☐	☐	☐
Old/high mileage vehicle	☐	☐	☐
Long future vehicle life expectancy	☐	☐	☐
Classic status	☐	☐	
Cheap spare parts availability	☐	☐	
High DIY/bush mechanic potential	☐	☐	
Main dealer service history	☐		☐
Metallic paintwork	☐		☐
Acceptable colour	☐	☐	☐

Appendix 3

SAMPLE PRIVATE SALES RECEIPT

14 High Street
Some Place
Anytown
AB1 4YZ

1 12 2006

Received from Mr J. Smith of 21 The Rise, Hilltown, CD6 8 WX,

the sum of £1,500 (one thousand five hundred pounds) cash payment in full for

Land Rover Defender Registered number A987XYZ

Chassis number SALLHAMV7A1239876.

Sold as seen, tried and tested.

J. Smith

J. Smith (buyer)

A. Jones

A. Jones (seller)

The details obviously need to be amended to suit. Both parties need to sign and the document needs dating in case you need to prove the sale date in order to resolve a speed camera incident or a similar problem. If the vehicle is unroadworthy due to the lack of an MoT or some other problem add 'and to be transported away' after 'as seen and tested'. Make two copies, keep one, and give the other to the purchaser with the section of the registration document that's theirs to take.

Appendix 4

VEHICLE INSPECTION CHECKLIST

- Body exterior
- Engine compartment
- Electrical/controls
- Interior and luggage compartment
- Front suspension/steering
- Clutch/transmission – manual
- Rear suspension and underframe
- Wheels and tyres
- Exhaust system
- Fuel system
- Brakes
- Road test
- Final check

Body exterior	Pass/fail	Notes or reason for fail
1 Panel condition/alignment		
2 Paintwork		
3 Exterior trim		
4 Glass		
5 Bumpers/number plates		
6 Door locks/operation		
7 Fuel filler cover/petrol cap		
8 Chassis numbers and VIN tags		
9 Body damage		
10 Past repair – poor workmanship evidence		
11 Corrosion		
12 Mudflaps		

Engine compartment

		Pass/fail	Notes or reason for fail
13	Coolant level		
14	Coolant leaks		
15	Antifreeze		
16	Radiator/cap		
17	Hoses/pipes		
18	Drive belts		
19	Water pump		
20	Power steering fluid level		
21	Clutch fluid level		
22	Brake fluid level		
23	Engine oil level		
24	External leaks (engine)		
25	Engine mountings		
26	Fuel injection		
27	Turbo/supercharger		
28	Fuel pump/pipes		
29	Accelerator linkage		
30	Body panels and structure		
31	Bonnet catch		
32	Bonnet hinges		
33	Cold starting		
34	Fast idle (cold)		
35	Noise level (cold)		
36	Excess fumes/smoke		

Electrical/controls

		Pass/fail	Notes or reason for fail
37	Starting system/ignition lock		
38	Battery charging system		
39	Headlights		
40	Sidelights		
41	Rear lights/number plate lights		
42	Stop lights		
43	Indicators/hazard lights		
44	Reverse/fog lights		
45	Auxiliary lights		
46	Panel lights		
47	Mirrors (electric)		
48	Switches/controls		
49	Instrument/controls function		
50	Horn		
51	Radio/cassette/CD/aerial		
52	Heater fan/controls		
53	Air conditioning operation		
54	Door locking		
55	Window/sunroof operation		
56	Wipers/washers		
57	Headlamp washer/headlamp wiper		

Interior and luggage compartment

		Pass/fail	Notes or reason for fail
58	Steering wheel/adjustment		
59	Seat upholstery		
60	Seat mechanism		
61	Seat belts		

Interior and luggage compartment (continued)

		Pass/fail	Notes or reason for fail
62	Carpets		
63	Door trim panels		
64	Door fittings/operation		
65	Door seals/hinges		
66	Interior sills		
67	Headlining/visors		
68	Sunroof		
69	Dash panel (condition)		
70	Cigarette lighter		
71	Mirrors – internal		
72	Rear parcel shelf		
73	Boot/tailgate lock		
74	Luggage area trim/condition		
75	Illumination lights		
76	Tool kit etc		
77	Soft Top material and function.		
78	Rain cover if present (Freelander)		

Front suspension/steering

		Pass/fail	Notes or reason for fail
79	Engine underside leakage		
80	Steering joints/ball joints		
81	Steering rack/box		
82	Chassis members		
83	Power steering		
84	Wheel hubs/bearings		
85	Springs/suspension unit		
86	Pipes/hoses		
87	Dampers (conditions/leaks)		
88	Gaiters		
89	Body mountings		
90	Suspension arms/mountings		
91	Tie bars/anti roll bars		
92	Corrosion protection		
93	Corrosion – floor/chassis/sills		

Clutch/transmission – manual

		Pass/fail	Notes or reason for fail
94	Fluid/oil leaks		
95	Cables/adjustment		
96	Hydraulic system		
97	Linkage (wear)		
98	Casings		
99	Mountings		
100	Driveshaft assemblies		
101	Universal/sliding joints		
102	Backlash		
103	Gaiters		
104	Propshaft(s)		
105	Bearings/supports		

Rear suspension and underframe

		Pass/fail	Notes or reason for fail
106	Springs/suspension unit		
107	Anti-roll bar		
108	Dampers/bushes		
109	Suspension fixings		
110	Location rod/fixings		
111	Bump stops		
112	Wheel hubs/bearings		
113	Pipes/hoses		
114	Body mountings		
115	Chassis members		
116	Corrosion protection		
117	Corrosion – floor/chassis		

Wheels and tyres

		Pass/fail	Notes or reason for fail
118	Wheel rims		
119	Wheel trims		
120	Front right tyre		
121	Front left tyre		
122	Rear right tyre		
123	Rear left tyre		
124	Spare		

Exhaust system

		Pass/fail	Notes or reason for fail
125	Manifold		
126	Pipes		
127	Silencer(s)/catalyst		
128	Heat shields/mountings		
129	Joints/couplings		
130	System condition		

Fuel system

		Pass/fail	Notes or reason for fail
131	Tank		
132	Tank fixings		
133	Fuel lines		
134	Breather pipes		
135	Evidence of leaks		

Brakes

		Pass/fail	Notes or reason for fail
136	Master cylinder security		
137	Fluid leaks		
138	Servo/power system		
139	Flexible hoses		
140	Pipes/connections		
141	Discs/pads (if visible)		
142	Hand/parking brake operation/adjustments		
143	Hand/parking brake linkage		
144	Pedal/linkage		

Road test

		Pass/fail	Notes or reason for fail
145	Engine – performance		
146	Engine – noise		
147	Excess smoke		
148	Overheating evidence		
149	Gearbox operation/noise level		
150	Auto changes/kickdown		
151	Final drive operation/noise level		
152	Clutch operation		
153	Four-wheel drive operation		
154	Cooling fan operation if hot enough		
155	Instrument/controls function		
156	Steering wheel alignment		
157	Steering effort		
158	General steering/handling		
159	Footbrake operation		
160	Hand/parking brake operation		
161	Suspension noise		
162	Road holding/stability		
163	Hot restarting		
164	Warning lights		
165	Cruise control		

Final check

		Pass/fail	Notes or reason for fail
166	Leaks – fluid		

Appendix 5

1979 SALE OF GOODS ACT

Factsheet and frequently asked questions

(© Crown Copyright 2006)

Subject:
Sale of Goods Act, Faulty Goods.

Relevant or Related Legislation:
Sale of Goods Act 1979.
Supply of Goods and Services Act 1982.
Sale and Supply of Goods Act 1994.
The Sale and Supply of Goods to Consumers Regulations 2002.

Key Facts:

- Wherever goods are bought they must 'conform to contract'. This means they must be as described, fit for purpose and of satisfactory quality (ie not inherently faulty at the time of sale).
- Goods are of satisfactory quality if they reach the standard that a reasonable person would regard as satisfactory, taking into account the price and any description.
- Aspects of quality include fitness for purpose, freedom from minor defects, appearance and finish, durability and safety.
- It's the seller, not the manufacturer, who is responsible if goods don't conform to contract.
- If goods don't conform to contract at the time of sale, purchasers can request their money back 'within a reasonable time'. (This isn't defined and will depend on circumstances.)
- For up to six years after purchase (five years from discovery in Scotland) purchasers can demand damages (which a court would equate to the cost of a repair or replacement).
- A purchaser who is a consumer, ie isn't buying in the course of a business, can alternatively request a repair or replacement.
- If repair and replacement aren't possible or too

costly, then the consumer can seek a partial refund, if they have had some benefit from the goods, or a full refund if the fault/s have meant they have enjoyed no benefit.

- In general, the onus is on all purchasers to prove the goods did not conform to contract (eg were inherently faulty) and should have reasonably lasted until this point in time (ie perishable goods don't last for six years).
- If a consumer chooses to request a repair or replacement, then for the first six months after purchase it will be for the retailer to prove the goods did conform to contract (eg were not inherently faulty).
- After six months and until the end of the six years, it's for the consumer to prove the lack of conformity.

Frequently asked questions (FAQs)

Q1. What's an inherent fault?

Q2. Do I only have rights for 30 [or some other number] days after purchase?

Q3. Do all goods have to last six (or five) years?

Q4. I know I can demand my money back within a 'reasonable time' but how long is that?

Q5. After the 'reasonable time has passed', what can I do?

Q6. Is it true that I have to complain to the manufacturer?

Q7. What can I do to claim damages or if the retailer won't honour my rights?

Q8. The retailer has claimed that a repair is 'disproportionately costly' and insists I accept a replacement as an alternative. Must I accept this?

Q9. Neither repair nor replacement are possible. What can I do?

Q10. What will the 'reversed burden of proof' mean for the consumer

Q1. What is an inherent fault?

A fault present at the time of purchase. Examples are:

- an error in design so that a product is manufactured incorrectly
- an error in manufacturing where a faulty component was inserted.

The 'fault' may not become apparent immediately but it was there at the time of sale and so the product was not of satisfactory standard.

Q2. Do I only have rights for 30 (or some other figure) days after purchase?

No. Depending on circumstances, you might be too late to have all your money back after this time, but the trader will still be liable for any breaches of contract, such as the goods being faulty. In fact, the trader could be liable to compensate you for up to six years.

Q3. Are all goods supposed to last six (or five) years?

No, that's the limit for bringing a court case in England and Wales (five years from the time of discovery in Scotland's case). An item only needs to last as long as it's reasonable to expect it to, taking into account all the factors. An oil filter would usually not last longer than a year but that wouldn't mean it was unsatisfactory.

Q4. I know I can demand my money back within a 'reasonable time' but how long is that?

The law doesn't specify a precise time as it will vary for most sales contracts as all the factors need to be taken into account to be fair to all sides.

Q5. After the 'reasonable time' has passed, what can I do?

You may seek damages, which would be the amount of money necessary to have the goods repaired or replaced. Frequently retailers will themselves offer repair or replacement. But, if you're a consumer (not making the purchase in the course of a business) you have the statutory right to seek a repair or replacement as an alternative to seeking damages.

Q6. Is it true that I have to complain to the manufacturer?

No. You bought the goods from the trader, not the manufacturer, and the trader is liable for any breaches of contract (unless he was acting as the manufacturer's agent).

Q7. What can I do to claim damages or if the retailer won't honour my rights?

The Small Claims Court procedure provides the means to bring a claim, for up to £5,000 (in England and Wales), at modest cost and without the need for a solicitor. Your local Citizens Advice Bureau can advise on how to make a claim.

Q8. The retailer has said that a repair is 'disproportionately costly' and insists I accept a replacement as an alternative. Must I accept this?

Yes, and vice versa if you request a replacement and this is 'disproportionately costly'. However, remember any remedy has to be carried out 'without significant inconvenience' and within a 'reasonable time' for the consumer. Remember that you could also seek damages instead.

Q9. Neither repair nor replacement of the goods are possible. What can I do?

You may either pursue the old route of damages or a partial or full refund. Probably either would give you exactly the same amount of money. You'd seek a full refund in scenarios such as those where you had enjoyed absolutely no benefit from the goods. If you had benefited from them then you'd seek a partial refund as a fair remedy. This is exactly the reasoning that would be employed if you sought damages.

Q10. What does the 'reversed burden of proof' mean for the consumer?

It means that for the first six months the consumer need not produce any evidence that a product was inherently faulty at the time of sale. If a consumer is seeking any other remedy the burden of proof remains with him/her.

In such a case, the retailer will either accept there was an inherent fault, and will offer a remedy, or he will dispute that it was inherently flawed. If the latter, when he inspects the product to analyse the cause, he may, for example, point out impact damage or stains that would be consistent with it having been mistreated in such a way as to bring about the fault.

This reversal of the usual burden of proof only applies when the consumer is seeking a repair or replacement. After the first six months the onus of proof is again on the consumer.

Further Guidance on Sale of Goods and Services Law:

For consumers: www.dti.gov.uk/ccp/topics1/guide/sogconsumerguide.pdf

For traders: www.dti.gov.uk/ccp/topics1/guide/sogtraderguide05.pdf

Index

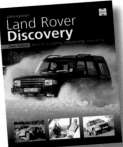
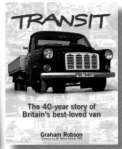
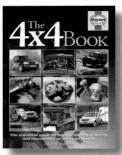
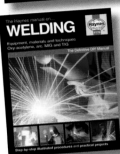
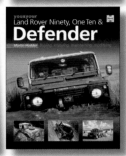

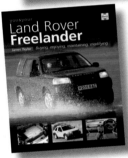

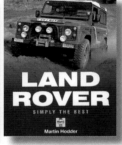

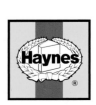